Helping Physicians Become Great Managers and Leaders

Helping Physicians Become Great Managers and Leaders

STRATEGIES THAT WORK

LAURA AVAKIAN

HEALTH FORUM, INC.
An American Hospital Association Company
Chicago

AHA and American Hospital Association are service marks of the American Hospital Association and are used under license by Health Forum, Inc.

Printed in the United States of America   11/10

Cover design by Jennifer Linton

ISBN: 978-1-55648-376-9   Item Number: 108106

Library of Congress Cataloging-in-Publication Data
Avakian, Laura.
   Helping physicians become great managers and leaders : strategies that work / Laura Avakian.
       p. cm.
   Includes bibliographical references and index.
   ISBN 978-1-55648-376-9 (alk. paper)
   1. Physician executives. 2. Leadership   I. Title.
RA972.A927 2010
610.68–dc22   2010018427

Discounts on bulk quantities of books published by Health Forum, Inc., are available to professional associations, special marketers, educators, trainers, and others. For details and discount information, contact Health Forum, Inc., 155 North Wacker Drive, Suite 400, Chicago, IL 60606 (Phone: 1-800-242-2626).

For Steve

Contents

List of Figures and Appendixes

About the Author

Laura Avakian is one of the leading human resources professionals in the United States. Following a thirty-year career as an executive in prestigious health care and higher-education organizations, Ms. Avakian now consults nationwide with organizations and individuals to enhance their personal, professional, and corporate effectiveness.

Before starting her consulting practice, she held positions as vice president of human resources for the Massachusetts Institute of Technology and senior vice president of human resources for the Beth Israel Deaconess Medical Center and its parent corporation, CareGroup. Under Ms. Avakian's leadership, her employers repeatedly won "best workplace" awards. Her innovative work focused on leadership development, executive coaching, and performance improvement.

She received her BA degree from the University of Missouri at Columbia and her MA degree from Northwestern University. She is past president of the American Society for Healthcare Human Resources Administration and the Northeast Human Resources Association. She has received the annual Award for Professional Excellence from the Society for Human Resource Management, the highest honor given by that international organization of more than 250,000 members.

A frequent speaker on management effectiveness and organizational transformation, Ms. Avakian has authored numerous articles and book chapters. She has served on the boards of both for-profit and not-for-profit companies and is currently on the board of directors of South Shore Hospital in suburban Boston.

Foreword

In 1967, the late John Lindsay, then mayor of New York City, inadvertently arranged my first job as a manager. Columbia University had announced that it was building a gymnasium in Harlem for its constituency but forgot that the surrounding community might want a voice in that decision. Riots ensued. When the dust settled, Lindsay suggested strongly that Columbia make amends by ending its affiliation with Bellevue Hospital, where I was to be chief resident in medicine, and bringing its resources to Harlem Hospital, then a forlorn, understaffed, and under-resourced institution in the heart of Harlem. So, on July 1, 1968, I found myself in Harlem leading fifty-five medical residents on wards that had only six the day before. Half were white, including eighteen idealistic graduates of Columbia's College of Physicians and Surgeons. The other half were a mix of African Americans and black Africans, most of whom never had been north of Washington, DC, and some freshly arrived as refugees from Biafra, Nigeria. My preparation for leadership consisted only of leading my college orchestra, and I needed help quickly.

Two weeks into the job, exhausted, depressed, and mired in chaos, I got my first lesson from a human resources (HR) manager. Vivian Dorsett, a tall and commanding black nurse who had long been the senior administrator of Harlem Hospital's department of medicine, grabbed my arm and pulled me into her office. Glaring, she sat me down and boomed something like: "Delbanco, you can either go on trying to have everyone love you, or you can get the job done. You had better pick option two, and that means you'll have to make some tough decisions. And make sure they're color blind!" Those few words turned me around 180 degrees, and I went on to have the most exciting and rewarding year of my professional life.

It wasn't the last time I needed HR help. After two years in the army, I came to what was then Boston's Beth Israel Hospital (now Beth Israel Deaconess Medical Center) to try to change the way the outpatient clinics worked and to help primary care earn a seat at the academic table. That service evolved over the next thirty-nine years into a delivery system serving 40,000 patients, an educational program that attracted many young doctors into primary care, and a complex clinical and health services research effort. I stopped running the show after its first thirty years and am now trying to play professor as one of more than 110 faculty in a $200 million enterprise. Writing these few words gives me a chance to look back and think about how access to remarkable human resources management helped shape my career for many of those thirty years.

In 1971, the Beth Israel "personnel department" seemed designed perfectly to stand in the way of progress. The rules were simple and singular: "You can't do that!" My colleagues and I were invariably slowed down or "spanked" for our efforts. Strange dictates emerged out of nowhere, meetings were pervasive, and all too often nothing got done.

Laura Avakian arrived in 1980 to take charge of what was now "human resources." At about that time, my doctor colleagues and I had crafted an eloquent petition denouncing a decision that prevented one of our nurses from receiving a raise we strongly recommended. Once again, I found myself summoned to an office. I arrived, accompanied by my second in command. A ridiculously young, almost baby-faced, woman sat us down on a couch that was to become famous in the hospital. First she led us through fair labor practices, which meant we were never to sign another petition. Then she effortlessly fashioned a plan that proved a win-win solution for all concerned. Our nurse was rewarded, equity for her peers was preserved, and guidelines for resolving similar issues in the future emerged.

Throughout the hospital, human resources practices changed with lightning speed. Almost overnight, we found ourselves privileged to have an HR department that became a safety net to everyone, from the hourly workers who kept our hospital clean to the chief executive officer and department chairs. Laura and her newly hired and trained colleagues guided us, listened to our ideas, and became our allies rather than our enemies. And her HR department quickly earned fame throughout the United States. Our hospital was honored time and again as "one of the best places to work," and Laura was recognized with a prize as the outstanding HR manager nationally, joining individuals from the likes of IBM and General Electric.

Why is her book so useful? When it comes to working with doctors, the job for HR managers isn't easy. Doctors in general are quite clever. At the very least, we have to get a lot of As on our way to and through medical school, and some say we are often too intelligent for our jobs. But whatever the reason for the HR manager's difficulty, we often make the highly unintelligent assumption that we can do everything well. Human resources decisions in particular often prove to be our downfall.

As this book shows clearly, good HR management is complicated, and the right decisions often seem counterintuitive. Time and again I would go into Laura's office quite sure that my decision A would be blessed, only to emerge convinced that her decision B was correct. David Segal, one of my greatest teachers at Columbia Medical School, taught my fellow students and me never to be embarrassed to take notes, and many years later that suggestion was put to good use in Laura's office. It became a standing rule in our hospital that one always enter her office with paper and pencil firmly in hand. Her words seemed crystal clear, logical, and always orderly. But you had to write them down, because the second you left her office you realized it was virtually impossible to recreate them. That was the clearest evidence that she is brilliant. It's always those special minds that make things seem simple until you try to recreate them.

That's the beauty of this book: Sage advice is close at hand. I suggest that, whatever type of leader you are, you first read it through in its entirety. Each chapter poses difficult questions, but each also provides the best answers. You'll realize both that this managing job is not easy and that a bit of preventive medicine can save the day. And, finally, you'll benefit from many of the notes taken in Laura Avakian's office by legions of managers that are herein written down. Would that that had been the case when I was running my show!

Tom Delbanco, MD
Koplow-Tullis Professor of General
Medicine and Primary Care
Harvard Medical School, Beth Israel
Deaconess Medical Center

Preface

As vice president of human resources, I thought I had heard every quirky request imaginable. But working late at my desk one evening, I was visited by two physicians—co-chairs of a medical unit—who asked for something that left me speechless: "We just learned the hospital gives on-call pay to employees who come in after hours," they said. "We have a technician who comes in all the time to fix some equipment, and we've never paid him anything extra." As I began to explain the policy, they stopped me and shook their heads. "He doesn't want any money," said one of the doctors, "because he would have to pay more alimony. But he would very much like to have a Harley. Can you arrange that, please?"

While the request for a Harley-Davidson motorcycle on behalf of an employee seems ludicrous on the surface, it was not unreasonable to the physicians who wanted a compensation solution to fit the circumstances of a valued employee. They were not interested in hearing about eligibility requirements, definitions of types of pay, forms, documentation, equity, or the Fair Labor Standards Act. They had diagnosed a problem, found a solution, and expected staff to implement it. Those physician managers, like many others, were oblivious to what we longtime administrators see as the nuts and bolts of management.

It is that disconnect and my great admiration for doctors that brought me to write this book. I have worked with physicians for many years. As a result of my experience, I offer the following generalizations about them:

- Each and every one of them is enormously intelligent.
- They are quick studies, who are reading the last paragraph while most of us are finishing the first.

- They are analytical; trained to evaluate problems; and, while they may seek input from a colleague, make autonomous judgments that they expect staff to carry out.

- Most of all, they are deeply committed to their patients. Those in research are equally devoted to finding cures for those who suffer.

Why Physicians Are Unprepared to Be Managers

Physicians' work is noble, and most of society views doctors with awe and expectation. Yet many physicians are less than effective, even disastrous, when they attempt to lead an organization and direct the work of other people.

Their lack of management skill may be explained by a number of reasons. Michael Rosenblatt, MD, former dean of Tufts University School of Medicine and a Merck & Co. executive, says physicians are not socialized the same as most people. "For many of them, their path to medical school starts early. Their mothers tell them that they are really smart and should become doctors. The aspiring physician then is allowed to focus almost all his or her efforts on studying, an individual effort. Then in medical school, the focus is on the patient, and the physician emerges as something of a lone ranger." When Rosenblatt observes a medical resident interviewing a patient of the same age, he is struck by the difference in their life experience. "The patient has been in the world for a while; the doctor is just learning to connect socially."

Further, physicians are trained to think independently and act autonomously. The skills that are so important in the diagnosis and treatment of patients are almost contradictory to those needed by managers: teamwork, collaboration, and deference to the leadership of colleagues with less medical knowledge but more "street smarts."

It is not uncommon for physicians to be appointed to their first management job when they are in their forties or fifties.

Most step into these roles with the idea of staying close to their patients and improving the systems of their care. They understand that they will be "the boss" but have minimal knowledge of the activities that make up most management jobs. They have never prepared agendas, conducted meetings, put together budgets, or hired or evaluated staff. Suddenly, they are sitting across the table from thirty-five-year-olds who already have a decade of experience in these areas and are speaking what seems like a foreign language that is peppered with terms like *ROI, on-boarding,* and *strategic planning.* What are they talking about, and what does it have to do with caring for patients?

How Administrators Teach and Support Physician Managers

Physician managers do not have to learn everything about the functioning of health care organizations to be successful leaders. But anyone in charge of directing others needs to understand the fundamentals of management, which this book provides. Happily, many doctors in leadership roles are supported by administrative colleagues who teach them much of what they need to know about policies and best practices.

While doctors, especially those new to supervisory jobs, will find the book pertinent, it is largely directed to those individuals who are the teachers, business partners, and "translators" for these physicians. Its intent is to help both the physician and the administrative ally determine who should perform which tasks and how to communicate with each other and the staff. It also guides both to resources within and outside the organization in supporting an education in management.

The book is also for administrators with organization-wide responsibilities in nonclinical areas—human resources, finance, facilities, operations, legal, marketing, and public affairs. These professionals need to understand the physician's mind-set, skills, and objectives and assist him or her in performing managerial tasks and achieving his or her goals, even if it means finding a way to get a motorcycle for a valued employee.

Each chapter begins with an anecdote related to the advice that follows. While the situations and dilemmas are true, drawn from my own and my colleagues' experiences, the names of the people and the places are fictitious. Although the focus is on the skills and knowledge gaps of the new physician manager, the real lessons emerge from the successes of the wonderful doctors and administrators who are the role models for effective leadership.

Physicians have so much of what it takes to become exceptional health care leaders. They keep the rest of us focused on the patient and are eager advocates for improving the systems of care delivery. It is a privilege to work with and for physicians, and this book is dedicated to furthering the belief that we have much to teach and learn from each other.

Laura Avakian
Hull, Massachusetts
March 1, 2010

Acknowledgments

I am deeply indebted to these physicians for their assistance in writing this book:

- Mitchell T. Rabkin, MD, my manager and mentor, who led Boston's Beth Israel Hospital to greatness for many decades and established the health system CareGroup
- Michael Rosenblatt, MD, who has held distinguished leadership roles in health care, academia, and private industry
- Tom Delbanco, MD, who is a pioneer in primary care and an innovator in developing systemized ways to involve patients in their care and who, for years, urged me to write this book

I am equally indebted to these administrative colleagues for their stories and examples of how to model effective partnerships with physicians:

- Richard Aubut, RN, president of South Shore Hospital, Weymouth, Massachusetts
- Robert Riney, chief operating officer of the Henry Ford Health System, Detroit
- Judy Hodgson, senior vice president of culture and people at PeaceHealth, Bellevue, Washington
- Brandon Melton, senior vice president of human resources at the Lifespan health system, Providence, Rhode Island
- Sarah O'Neill, director of ambulatory operations and special projects, and Jo Ayoub, director of organizational development, at Beth Israel Deaconess Medical Center, Boston

I also thank my sisters, Lynn Hawkins and Jane Oakley, for their editing suggestions; my brothers, Robb and Ed McClary, and friend Matt Hollingshead for their technical assistance; my mother, Elizabeth McClary, for her steadfast encouragement; and my husband, Steve Avakian, who provided his journalistic expertise and loving support throughout this journey.

And finally, I am grateful to Richard Hill, editorial director at AHA Press, who has nurtured this book with patient oversight and gentle direction.

Helping Physicians Become
Great Managers and Leaders

1

Getting the Physician Manager
Off to a Good Start

Help the newly appointed
physician manager understand
and become oriented to a role
very different from doctoring.

Beverly Lane, MD, was the unanimous choice of the selection committee charged with recommending a new chief for the dermatology division. Having graduated summa cum laude with undergraduate and master's degrees from prestigious colleges, she went on to medical school, where she also excelled. She considered a career in research but so enjoyed the patient care experience during her residency that she joined the staff of the department at City General. In addition to her impeccable academic credentials and published research, she was admired by her peers for her teaching capability and was well liked by both patients and staff. Her selection as chief brought stature to the department within and outside the hospital.

A few months into the job, Dr. Lane began to experience some difficulties. She was highly stressed; she was continuing to see patients and take on-call duty, and though she had reduced her clinical schedule, she complained to me that she had no time to breathe. She said her days were consumed with meetings, many of which seemed pointless to her. She actually walked out of a presentation on the new patient scheduling system. She also asked for a month's extension for submitting her department budget. Normally a calm and soft-spoken person, Dr. Lane found herself snapping at her administrative assistant. In our meeting last week, she told me that she thought she made a mistake in taking the job. "I am miserable, and I'm making everybody else miserable," she said.

Although I didn't say it out loud, I was tempted to agree with her. Perhaps we had both overestimated her capabilities. Instead I urged her to give it more time. I also told her that it had taken me a number of years to get comfortable working on management issues instead of seeing patients, but now I wouldn't trade my job as CEO for anything.

She left my office with a commitment to keep trying, and I vowed to myself that I would try to get her some help. But first, I'd better let the chairman of the board know we may have a problem here.

--------------------------------Robert Hull, MD, Chief Executive Officer

Introduction

A physician's first management job can be either a bewildering and disappointing experience or one that is gratifying and enjoyable. Usually, it is both, at least to some degree. The better prepared a physician is to perform managerial tasks, the more likely he or she is to succeed at the role and find it personally rewarding. However, many doctors have had little or no experience in heading complex organizations and directing the work of other people. Additionally, the characteristics that made them successful clinicians—autonomous and speedy decision making and a focus on individual production—are diametrically opposed to the talents they need to be successful managers. Therefore, in assuming these leadership roles, physicians must *unlearn* how they approach their work as well as acquire a completely new set of skills.

This chapter addresses four aspects of helping physicians get off to a good start when they become managers: understanding the role of a manager, orienting a physician to a management position, supporting physician managers in their leadership roles, and resources available to physicians and their administrative partners.

Understanding the Role of a Manager

Did Beverly Lane know what work she would be doing when she accepted the position as chief of dermatology? Clearly an intelligent person, outstanding in her field, and familiar with the hospital, she no doubt has a clear vision of what the division can achieve in terms of patient care and research. But she did not anticipate either some of the tasks she would need to perform as manager of the division or the time it would take to carry them out. What she and the chief executive officer (CEO) of the hospital fear may be a mismatch of her talents with the job may, in fact, be a lack of understanding of what the job is and what she needs to do to prepare for it.

The first aspect of management that must be understood is that the manager defines the goals to be accomplished and then oversees the work of others in achieving them. This step requires the manager to have a plan and then to know what capabilities staff need to carry it out. Richard Aubut, president of South Shore Hospital in Weymouth, Massachusetts, says that some physicians fail as managers because they cannot put together a plan. "Some think that asking for a piece of equipment is a plan," he says. "Or they see creating a budget as a goal rather than as a tool to use in planning and prioritizing work."

There is little in a physician's training that would teach him or her the skills of planning and budgeting. Thus, those whose job it is to orient physician leaders to their role need to find ways to support them in this learning. Available resources to do so are covered later in this chapter.

Another necessary skill is time management. Dr. Lane does not want to give up her patient contact and is frustrated with the amount of time she must spend in meetings that are meaningless to her. Many chiefs of clinical departments continue to see patients in addition to directing the work of the unit, so that factor may not be a problem. But how that work is balanced with other responsibilities is an issue. Dr. Lane's schedule is driving her; ideally, she should be driving the schedule. In planning her time, she needs to be clear about priorities and to determine whether she or someone else is the right person to perform certain tasks or attend certain meetings.

As individual contributors, physicians and other clinicians focus on the patient in front of them at the time. They may follow a schedule that has been established for them, but they are working very much "in the moment." Their priority is the immediate care to be given, not the activity of all the other clinicians, the condition of equipment and facilities, or the money and talent that will be required for care to be delivered over the next year or next decade. So the question that physician managers need to ask themselves is not "What is my work?" but "What is the overall work of the unit for which I am responsible?" The answer to this question forms the foundation of a business plan and helps the manager think about priorities. It also requires that he or she begin thinking about long-term goals and work needs and who will be available to perform them.

As the manager understands that his or her job is to get work done through other people, he or she will also realize that the job requires hiring qualified people, delegating work to them, monitoring their performance, dealing with their problems, and inspiring and rewarding them. These topics, which are the subjects of subsequent chapters, are the core responsibilities of a manager. The leaders of the hospital must carefully consider how to evaluate the capabilities of candidates for management jobs as well as how to teach these skills to physicians and others who need to acquire them in order to do the job for which they have been hired.

The role of the manager is summarized in figure 1-1.

Orienting a Physician to a Management Position

No physician would ever think of diagnosing and treating a patient before he or she had gone to medical school, yet many

Figure 1-1. The Role of the Manager

The manager is responsible for:

- Articulating a vision
- Creating a plan to achieve the vision
- Establishing priorities
- Determining the tasks required to carry out the plan
- Delegating responsibilities and tasks to others
- Hiring qualified staff
- Monitoring, evaluating, and rewarding performance
- Helping solve staff's problems
- Acknowledging success and using it to advance the vision

start jobs as directors or administrators without any training or formal education in management. Some hospitals that promote or hire physicians into such roles allow search committees to evaluate candidates on the basis of their clinical, academic, and research accomplishments and their personality traits without thoroughly vetting their managerial competence and experience. And physicians, like everyone else, not knowing what they do not know, may assume that their previous achievements will translate into future success as a manager.

A number of activities must take place to ensure a physician becomes a successful manager; they include the following:

- Candidates for these jobs are screened for managerial competence, and their experiences in prior leadership roles are researched and evaluated.
- A formal orientation program is established that sets expectations for performance, introduces the physician to the culture and values of the organization, and familiarizes him or her with relevant policies and resources.
- Mentors are identified to guide and counsel new physician managers.

■ Physicians are supported in obtaining a master of business administration (MBA) degree and/or attending professional seminars or workshops on leadership development.

Conducting an effective hiring process is the first important step for a health care organization to take in orienting the selected physician to his or her new role. The job description used by the search committee should clearly state the managerial competencies required, such as those needed to perform the functions delineated in figure 1-1. Candidates should be screened for these competencies, and the interviewers should ask the candidates to give examples of how and where they have demonstrated these skills in the past. While they may not have been hospital or practice managers before, the candidates should be asked about leadership roles they may have had with a church, a community group, or another kind of business.

Aubut describes hiring physician managers at South Shore Hospital as an inclusive process. He wants to know how they will fit with the organization's culture and how they will solve problems. "We have candidates meet a lot of people in the process," he says. "We give them a tour, have them meet all the VPs [vice presidents], and deliberately bulk them up with reading material. We also invite them for a meal with the senior management team to watch how they think on their feet. We see if they approach problem solving from the perspective of the doctor or the perspective of the patient. If it's the doctor's perspective, that is the end of the interview."

Although large search committees can be cumbersome, they may serve to transition the physician into his or her new role in that those who have participated in an individual's selection usually feel they have a stake in that person's success. Thus, the newly hired manager starts with a group of supporters and colleagues who serve as willing sources of information and assistance.

Once the manager is on board, he or she should attend the formal orientation for all new employees that the hospital or health system offers. Here one receives general information about such topics as the organization's history, the scope and size of its services, employee benefits, and safety protocols. Frequently employees are given a tour of the facilities and may meet the president or other members of administration. Additionally, the on-boarding process for managers should include a highly individualized orientation that is developed by the department administrator in conjunction with the physician manager's immediate supervisor.

At the Cleveland Clinic Foundation, the on-boarding process includes a significant set of activities that augments the new physicians' individual orientations. As reported in a winter 2009 article in *HR Pulse*, the program is part of a larger educational effort called the Cleveland Clinic Academy. The on-boarding activities take place over approximately six months and include introductions to people and the organizational culture; follow-up surveys after 90 days; and two full-day sessions called "Inside the Cleveland Clinic," where new staff meet with peers and Clinic leaders to discuss roles and the state of the organization.[1]

In hospitals or health systems generally, an orientation schedule for a new chief, developed by the chief's administrative partner and reviewed by the president, might include the kinds of introductions and meetings noted in figure 1-2.

In addition to handling the welcomes and general introductions noted in figure 1-2, the administrative manager should arrange for the new chief to meet with people who are heading projects or programs that will affect the chief in the near term, such as those leading a new compliance or safety program, building project, or fund-raising initiative. An important way to welcome the chief is to include his or her spouse or partner in some of the activities. Given the intensity of health care leadership roles, the family is a much-needed source of support for all managers. Another useful approach is to designate an individual, usually a peer of the new physician manager, to be a mentor or

Figure 1-2. Orientation, Introductions, and Meetings

An orientation schedule for a new clinical chief might include the following:

- A coffee hour with all staff in the department
- A social event hosted by the president for all chiefs and spouses
- Introduction at a medical staff meeting
- Introduction at a board meeting
- Introduction at a senior management meeting
- Individual meetings with
  —the chief nursing officer
  —the chief financial officer (CFO)
  —the chief human resources officer
  —all VPs of operations and key services, such as legal and public affairs
- An opportunity to shadow staff in his or her department

even just a good informal source of answers to questions such as "Do I wear my lab coat or a suit when I meet the board?"

A comprehensive orientation is critical in getting a new manager off to a good start. While it helps acculturate him or her and provides a foundation for him or her to operate within the hospital's administrative structure, the orientation itself does not teach one to be a manager. It is important that those skills be learned through both didactic study and experience.

Aubut was a registered nurse with no management experience when he was hired as an assistant director of nursing. He soon realized he needed to learn the language of the CFO. "Nursing folks were saying it's all about quality; the CFO was saying it's all about money. I learned that if you couldn't translate that quality conversation into dollars and cents, it just sounded like whining." So he enrolled in an executive MBA program, taking courses on nights and weekends to acquire that knowledge. Similarly, Mitchell T. Rabkin, MD, president emeritus of Boston's Beth Israel Hospital, when asked whether he would have done anything differently during his several decades of leadership, replied, "I would have gone back to school for an MBA."

These two outstanding hospital leaders share another approach to learning about management: They read all the time. Both point to numerous books that have guided them on their leadership journeys, and both continue to read current literature about management. Most importantly, they success-fully integrate that knowledge into the day-to-day leadership of their organizations.

There is increasing recognition that physicians who are or who desire to become managers in health care organizations require a "new kind" of education. Today, more than fifty schools offer joint MD/MBA programs. One of the oldest pro-grams is offered at Tufts University School of Medicine, where the joint curriculum is embedded in four years of study. Former Tufts dean Michael Rosenblatt, MD, wrote in fall 2009 about the changing role of physicians: "Formerly it was standard pro-cedure for medical schools to educate their students with the idea that, once graduated, they would act as independent agents in their careers. That approach no longer makes sense. . . . Now it is more critical for physicians to be effective collaborators with their colleagues and co-workers. Doctors must be both team members and leaders to serve their patients well."[2] Information about joint degree programs can be found on the Web site of the National Association of MD/MBA Students, www.md-mba .org. Universities offer joint programs for MD/MHA (master of health administration) and MD/MPH (master of public health) degrees as well.

Supporting Physician Managers in Their Leadership Roles

It is important that physicians who are hired into management roles understand what the job is and how it differs from clinical roles. It is also crucial that they receive education and training in management and that they are fully oriented to their new roles. However, not every management task should be performed by a physician leader, either because it is not the best use of his or her time or because others can do it more efficiently due to their unique skills or place in the organization.

The optimum leadership model for a clinical unit, service, or program is one whereby responsibilities are shared between a physician director and a nonphysician administrator, sometimes called a product line manager, department administrator, or business partner. In this model the two leaders need to have a common strategy and be committed to the same goals. Sarah Turner O'Neill, in her former role as administrator for Beth Israel Hospital's primary care teaching practice, describes the partnership this way: "I was best at billing, scheduling, overseeing day-to-day operations; the physician director brought the vision for the program and could talk about patient care with the other providers and convince them to follow a course of action in a way I never could."

Sharing overall responsibility but dividing up the management tasks also allows both to use their time more effectively, one of the problems that plagues Dr. Lane at the start of this chapter. For example, meetings are essential for effective communications and collaborative problem solving, but they are also time consuming. Meeting attendance may be divided to alleviate this concern. The physician manager should attend meetings of the clinical chiefs and the medical staff and participate in interdisciplinary meetings with the heads of nursing, pharmacy, laboratories, radiology, and so forth to deal with both strategic and operational issues. The department administrator should attend meetings of administrative department heads and those convened to deal with issues of budget, information systems, human resources policies, and facilities.

However, at times it is important to include physician managers in meetings where they will be directly affected by the outcome, even if the topic seems more administrative in nature. For example, a committee to decide capital acquisitions may be most effectively led by a physician. He or she can challenge the doctors' requests and at the same time help the finance staff to appreciate differences in the quality of equipment.

Physician managers should also participate in meetings where key personnel decisions are made. In one case, a decision to terminate a nursing assistant with a long, carefully documented history of poor performance was made by a nursing manager in conjunction with the department administrator and human resources. When the physician manager learned of the decision, he refused to support it, and it was not enacted. He had worked with the nursing assistant on occasion and thought her performance was "fine." He did not know her history, nor had he been aware of the discussions leading to the decision to terminate her. The result was bad for all involved—those who made the decision were demoralized, an unsuccessful employee continued to be unsuccessful, and the physician leader with lots of clout but too little information felt his team let him down.

O'Neill says that administrators need to anticipate that doctors may react this way and to work with them first. "Physicians are trained to be decisive," she says. "Everybody looks to them to say what should be done. It is difficult for them to think about a repeated pattern or about exceptions to rules. If I am mentoring new managers, I try to help them first understand the physician's way of looking at the world and then how to go about involving doctors in decisions."

In summary, the tasks that are best delivered by physician managers and those best performed by administrative managers are delineated in figures 1-3 and 1-4, respectively.

In addition, a number of tasks should be performed by the physician manager and administrative manager together. These are indicated in figure 1-5.

Figure 1-3. Tasks Best Performed by the Physician Manager

The physician manager is best suited for:

- Articulating a vision for the organizational unit
- Representing the unit when meeting with other clinicians in the hospital
- Participating on hospitalwide committees that benefit from clinical expertise
- Advising, evaluating, and rewarding physicians in the unit
- Resolving issues among the unit's clinical staff

Figure 1-4. Tasks Best Performed by the Administrative Manager

The administrative manager is best suited for:

- Overseeing the day-to-day operations of the unit
- Developing and monitoring the budget
- Recommending hires and other personnel actions
- Representing the unit when meeting with other administrative managers in the hospital
- Facilitating interactions between the physician manager and staff

Figure 1-5. Tasks Best Performed by Physician and Administrative Managers Together

The physician manager and administrative manager are most successful when they share responsibility for:

- Agreeing on goals and strategy
- Determining priorities and final budget
- Deciding new hires, promotions, and terminations of unit staff
- Deciding which manager should communicate which messages
- Presenting a united front and supporting each other's decisions

Resources Available to Physicians and Their Administrative Partners

Hospitals have access to numerous resources to support physicians as they step into management jobs. Many of these have been mentioned throughout this chapter. Following is a summary of the resources that are most helpful:

- Educational resources
  - —MD/MBA and MD/MHA programs
  - —Executive MBA programs
  - —Seminars and workshops offered by professional membership organizations
  - —Leadership development programs offered by the training and development department within the hospital
- Advice and coaching resources
  - —A peer who serves as mentor
  - —A professional executive coach
  - —Senior managers
  - —Human resources counselors

Conclusion

The most successful managers love their work. They like thinking about it and learning how to do it better. They recognize that management is an intellectual enterprise and that the principles of management theory are as substantive as those on which science is based. They also understand that one must continuously be open to new learning. One's own leadership development contributes to that of others and ultimately leads to a sense of gratification that comes from seeing his or her staff succeed. The skills and techniques needed for inclusive leadership are probed in the chapters ahead.

References

1. Anne Coulter, "On-Boarding at the Cleveland Clinic," *HR Pulse* (winter 2009): 18–20.

2. Michael Rosenblatt, "Teaching the Future," *Tufts Medicine* (fall 2009): 3.

2

Helping the Physician Manager Hire Staff

Avoid bad hiring decisions by understanding the selection process and conducting effective interviews and reference checks.

When I was promoted to chief of my division, I was immediately overwhelmed with the complexity of the budget I was given to manage and the time it was taking away from overseeing the clinical work that was, frankly, more important to me and more interesting. So I decided to hire a budget analyst to help me out.

I interviewed Debbie, who was recommended to me by one of the surgeons who plays golf with Debbie's dad. She was very personable and struck me as intelligent. During the interview I carefully explained the budget and what I felt needed to be done. I was very clear about the importance of accuracy and told her I needed a self-starter. She agreed with everything I said.

I don't know where it went wrong, but Debbie was a disaster. She didn't really seem to understand the budget, and it was full of errors. I found I was spending more time than ever on budget issues. When I tried to correct her, she blamed others on the staff for not giving her good data. On top of everything, she seemed to need every Friday off for some personal reasons.

By the time she finally quit, I had developed so many work-arounds that she was hardly touching the budget at all. I need the help, but now I'm gun-shy about making another [hiring] mistake.

--------------------Marvin Andrews, MD, Chief, Pulmonary Division

15

Introduction

Hiring people who will be successful in their job requires skill and planning. We are attracted to individuals who are highly recommended or who are easy to talk with, but they may or may not be the best candidate for the position or even capable of performing the required work. The hiring manager must fully understand the qualifications needed and thoroughly evaluate the applicants' fit with the requirements.

This chapter addresses five aspects of hiring: developing a comprehensive description of the job, locating qualified applicants, conducting the interview, checking references before making a job offer, and using available resources to assist in the hiring process.

Developing a Comprehensive Description of the Job

Dr. Andrews had a good idea of what kind of help he wanted, but did he articulate it fully and in writing? Did he even know what kind of education and experience would be necessary for a person to do the job well? Did he need a budget analyst or someone with another skill set?

Most hospitals have a formal process for preparing a written job description and presenting it in a prescribed format. It can be initiated by the department head or by an administrator who is charged with supporting that department. The draft description should be submitted to the human resources (HR) department, where it is reviewed for completeness and assigned a pay grade and an appropriate title. The HR staff also verify that the position is one of the budgeted complement of jobs or, if it is a new position, that it has been approved at the appropriate level.

To the impatient physician manager who feels desperate for help and eager to fill the position quickly, this process seems like a massive amount of bureaucracy and red tape. One employment manager recalls a doctor yelling at her: "Don't give me *process*, just get me a good secretary!"

While it is the responsibility of HR to respond in a timely manner and work closely with the physician or his or her administrator, one should not shortcut the process. If vital steps are left out, the following issues may arise:

- Insufficient thought given to the desired responsibilities and duties can result in the job not getting done or the wrong work being done. This situation further creates disappointment and conflict for both the employee and the manager.

- The job may be misclassified, resulting in the employee being paid too little or too much for the work performed.

- Inequities in volume of work and/or pay may result between the new employee and current staff, creating resentment and conflict.

- The job may not carry the correct title, creating confusion about the employee's role and place in the organization.

- The job description becomes the basis for performance appraisal after the employee is in the position for a period of time. If it is not accurate at the outset, how can an employee be fairly appraised later?

Locating Qualified Applicants

It is not known from Dr. Andrews' story whether he interviewed other candidates for the budget analyst job in addition to Debbie and, if he did, how he learned of them. It appears that in his eagerness to hand off the budget responsibilities, he jumped at the referral from a colleague who likely had little knowledge of the necessary job requirements. Personal referrals may in fact produce a qualified candidate and a successful employee, but they should undergo the same scrutiny and evaluation as other candidates for the position.

After the job description is approved and pay and title are established, the physician manager can expect HR to identify candidates and establish a general time frame for filling the position.

Most health care organizations have a system for posting available jobs on internal bulletin boards, the hospital's Web site, and/or external Internet job sites for a period of time. An HR recruiter generally screens candidates and refers qualified individuals to the hiring manager for an interview. Unless it is essential that someone already working in the hospital fill the posted position, the HR recruiter will begin to identify other possible sources of qualified applicants.

The typical sources beyond internal posting boards and the hospital's Web site are the following:

- *Advertising.* Help-wanted advertisements in newspapers and journals are used less frequently now than in the past. Today, both employers and job applicants are likely to use Web-based sites such as Monster.com or Craig's List. Most large newspapers also have Internet sites that contain job listings.

- *Employment or recruitment agencies.* The employer will likely pay a fee for an agency service, though in some cases the job applicants pay a fee to an agency to refer them.

- *Retained search.* For key positions, an employer may retain a search firm to identify candidates. The firm helps prepare the job description and often works with the hospital's search committee to determine criteria and to evaluate candidates. While fees of search firms vary, the employer can expect to pay an amount equal to 33 percent of the first year's salary of the individual who is hired.

- *Professional organizations.* Many organizations sponsor job listings for their members. The American Nurses Association, the Healthcare Financial Management Association, and the Society for Human Resource Management are a few examples.

- *Job fairs and career days.* These events are conducted to reach large numbers of potential candidates who may be contacted when job openings arise later. Sometimes they target a specific occupation such as nurses or administrative assistants; other times they are intended to attract broad groups such as "health professionals" or "technical professionals."

Deciding on the best sources of candidates for a position should be a collaborative process wherein the physician manager, the administrative liaison for the area, and the HR specialist all bring their unique knowledge to the discussion.

Here are some pitfalls to avoid:

- Do not use a more expensive recruitment source than is necessary to fill the vacancy. Retained search should be used only in cases when a national search is required or the skills needed are unique to the point where talent must be sought from those not in the job market.
- Do not spend the time or precious resources on advertising the position everywhere. Carefully target the sources most likely to yield solid candidates.
- Consider personal referrals. Current employees are often the best recruiters. They know the culture and their co-workers, and they have a vested interest in the success of their referral on the job. However, do not let emotion or loyalty be the determining factor in hiring. Personal referrals must be given the same scrutiny as other candidates.

Conducting the Interview

Dr. Andrews tells us what was discussed during the interview, and what we know about Debbie's part is that she agreed with him. While Debbie must have talked about her experience and qualifications, it is possible that Dr. Andrews did not delve deeply into them, perhaps taking them for granted, and used the interview to stress those aspects of the job that were important to him. It can be a disastrous mistake for the interviewer to dominate the interview and to take the applicant's concurrence with his or her statements as evidence of qualification for the job. The interviewer should speak for no more than 30 percent of the interview time, leaving the applicant 70 percent of the time to answer or initiate questions.

The following agenda shows how an effective thirty-minute interview might go:

2:00 to 2:04 PM *Opening: Physician manager initiates a welcoming conversation.*

Dr. Andrews: Welcome, Debbie. Thanks for coming in on such a cold day. Were you able to park close to the office?

Debbie: Thanks for seeing me. I took the bus here. I am really excited about this job.

2:05 to 2:07 PM *Physician manager sets expectations for the interview and asks the most important question first.*

Dr. Andrews: We only have thirty minutes together, and I'd like to spend that time finding out as much as possible about your experience and how this job might fit your career goals. I will make sure you have time to ask me any questions you might have.

First, have you had a chance to review the job description? Good. Tell me first how you became interested in financial operations and budgeting in particular. Did you study this area of finance in college?

2:08 to 2:10 PM *Applicant answers.*

Debbie: I actually received my degree in fine arts. I love painting and going to museums, stuff like that. But I really like numbers, too. I worked summers in my dad's office keeping his books. He owns some rental property, and I had to make sure all the rents came in and the bills were paid. There was a lot of detail to it.

2:11 to 2:12 PM *Physician manager probes.*

Dr. Andrews: How many accounts did you handle? Did you use Excel© spreadsheets or some other software to track the data?

Tell me more about the scope of that work and whether you have other financial experience.

2:13 to 2:15 PM *Applicant talks about experience.*

Debbie: Well, Dad only had three tenants, so I was able to keep everything in a notebook. I didn't have to use the computer, but I know how. I do e-mail all the time. Sometimes I had to go to the properties to pick up the rent checks. And it involved a lot of phone conversations. I made bank deposits and kept those records in a file. In my first job out of college, I worked at a camp for children, and I was responsible for keeping all its records straight, like which participants had paid their fees and which had not, whose health records were on file, and a lot of other details. I haven't worked in a hospital before, but I worked for a dentist, and I'm very good with people.

2:16 to 2:18 PM *Physician manager probes experience further and checks for compatibility with values and culture of the hospital.*

Dr. Andrews: I'd like to learn more about your work and what makes it satisfying to you. Tell me about your favorite job. What made it a positive experience? Also, tell me about a job experience—don't mention any names—that was unsatisfying or in which you felt you were not successful.

2:19 to 2:25 PM *Applicant tries to sell herself for the job.*

Debbie: Well, I've really liked all my jobs, pretty much. My most favorite was the children's camp. I felt like I taught them a lot, and it was so much fun being outside all summer. Their parents thanked me all the time. I don't think I've ever been unsuccessful at anything, but recently I worked in a dentist's office where I had to do many different things. I was supposed to greet patients and get their charts and arrange appointments and even straighten up the waiting room. It was just too busy and confusing, so I decided to look for something more satisfying.

2:26 to 2:27 PM *Physician manager gives her opportunity for questions.*

Dr. Andrews: You've been very forthright and thorough in answering my questions. In the few moments we have left, is there anything I can tell you about the job or the hospital?

2:28 to 2:29 PM *Applicant asks questions.*

Debbie: I was wondering about the hours of the job and how much vacation I would get. Also, is there any flexibility to work, like, a four-day workweek?

2:30 PM *Physician manager closes interview.*

Dr. Andrews: I believe our vacation policy provides for two weeks' vacation in the first year of employment. I'm sorry, but the job would require five regular eight-hour days each week.

I want to thank you for coming in. We are just beginning the interview process, and I plan to see other candidates. I should be candid with you and let you know that I expect to see others who have more direct budgeting experience. However, I'll make sure the human resources department stays in touch with you regarding our progress with the search. Thank you again.

Some points to take away from this interview include the following:

1. Dr. Andrews spoke no more than ten minutes during the thirty-minute interview.

2. He learned that Debbie had no specific educational preparation for the role and no direct experience with budgeting.

3. He learned that she gets the most satisfaction from people interaction, an opportunity the budget analyst job will not offer.

4. He learned that she has not worked with complex financial programs, does not have the necessary computer skills, and was frustrated with multitasking.

5. There was a strong suggestion that Debbie desired a four-day workweek, perhaps hinting at the possibility of Friday absences that would occur if hired.

6. Overall, Dr. Andrews could conclude by the end of the interview that Debbie is not well qualified for the job. He gave her candid feedback about her lack of relevant experience.

It is clear that Dr. Andrews would not have hired Debbie as a budget analyst had he conducted the interview as outlined above, which would have saved them both time and disappointment.

Tips for conducting the interview are provided in figure 2-1.

Checking References before Making a Job Offer

The comments of employment references should be considered with a healthy amount of skepticism. In some cases, a former employer will cite only an employee's strengths and successes and neglect to mention any problems or difficulties the employee may have had on the job. If the employee had been involuntarily terminated, a former employer may be even more reluctant to talk or write candidly about the circumstances, and sometimes termination agreements exist that preclude either party from commenting on job performance or reasons for termination. Employers have grown so concerned about possible legal action from disgruntled former employees that many will only verify dates of employment and position held.

Equally suspect are letters of recommendation that an applicant submits or brings to an interview. Again, a past employer may feel pressured to comment on only the positive aspects of an employee's work. Also, the hiring manager has no way of

Figure 2-1. Tips for the Interviewer

Follow a few simple rules to improve your interviewing technique:

- Limit your comments to no more than 30% of the total interview time.

- Do not ask questions about marital status, health, age, political or religious affiliation, plans to have children, or any other topic that is not relevant to the job to be performed. Ask open-ended questions that reveal an applicant's values and compatibility with your culture—questions about teamwork, attention to detail, commitment to stick with the job until it is finished, and so forth.

- Be friendly, offer a firm handshake, and look the applicant in the eye. Do not take phone calls or allow other interruptions during the interview.

knowing whether the recommender has the same standards of performance the candidate has.

So should one bother with references at all? Yes, if the information is obtained by a skilled reference auditor, such as an interviewer in the HR department. The auditor must be adept at assessing the qualifications of the information provider to offer a meaningful reference. He or she must also judge the quality of the information and its relevance to the job for which the applicant is being considered. References should be obtained in a phone conversation so the auditor has the opportunity to establish rapport with the former employer and ask follow-up questions. The kinds of questions to ask references are noted in figure 2-2.

Using Available Resources

The best source of help in the hiring process is the HR department. Its professionals will help prepare the job description, determine appropriate title and pay level, post the position internally, recommend sources of candidates, place advertisements,

Figure 2-2. Questions to Ask in a Reference Audit

1. What is your job? How long have you been doing this work?
2. What was your relationship with the candidate? How long did you work with him or her, and in what capacity?
3. What were the candidate's responsibilities in your organization?
4. What did he or she do best? What was his or her greatest achievement?
5. What did the candidate still need to learn at the time he or she left?
6. Why did he or she leave?
7. Describe the candidate's relationship with co-workers.
8. Of all the employees you have supervised, where would you rank this individual?
9. Would you rehire him or her in the same or a different capacity?
10. What haven't I asked you about the candidate that I should know?

screen resumes, conduct preliminary interviews, and perform reference audits.

The physician manager should also ask his or her administrative director—whether a hospital vice president who supports the department or the departmental administrator—to interview final candidates. Multiple perspectives are helpful in assessing a candidate's fit with the organization.

Conclusion

When carefully planned and skillfully conducted, the selection process can be an enjoyable experience that will result in hiring individuals who will be highly valued colleagues. The interview itself can be a delightful process of mutual discovery. Some of the author's favorite interview questions are shared in figure 2-3.

A well-constructed interview is the foundation of a good hiring decision. If the applicant is hired, the interview is also the first important step in orienting him or her to the culture and values of the organization and sets the stage for the way the manager and employee will work together.

Figure 2-3. Favorite Interview Questions

1. How would your best friend describe you?
2. What is the greatest challenge you have overcome in your life?
3. Who has inspired you the most in your life?
4. Describe a time when you were disappointed. How did you respond to the situation?
5. When have you led or given direction to other people? Tell me about the experience.
6. What is an accomplishment you want to achieve in your life that you haven't yet reached?
7. What do you do in your free time?
8. What is the best job you ever had, and why?
9. What is the worst job you ever had, and why?
10. If you come to work here, what will I know about you after three years that I don't know today?

3

Delegating Work to Others

**Assign work and grant
authority to make decisions.
Inclusive management develops staff
and produces better results.**

*I guess there is truth to that old saying that if you want something
done right, you have to do it yourself. It's not that my staff aren't
well intentioned. It's just that I have to give them very specific
instructions and then watch carefully to make sure the work is completed like I would do it. And then there are times I just don't get
the cooperation I need.*

*For example, as the new head of one of the ambulatory areas,
I could tell that patients were waiting too long to be seen, and I
felt we should quicken the process. I called a staff meeting and
told the clinicians to speed up their patient visits, and I told the
scheduler to spread out the appointments better. I also told the
receptionist to bring any patient complaints about waiting directly
to my attention.*

*The doctors grumbled that they didn't have enough time with
their patients as it was, and the scheduler wanted to do some kind
of elaborate study to see how long patients were actually waiting.
The receptionist complained that I was always busy when she tried
to track me down.*

*I finally just implored them all to do their best to try to make
it better. Everybody said they would, but that was six months ago,
and the wait times are worse than ever. I think I need to hire some
staff who "get it."*

--------Margot Baker, MD, Chief, the Ear, Nose, and Throat Clinic

Introduction

Delegating work so that others effectively achieve the desired results is a critical skill for any manager. Physicians new to management roles often do not bring this skill to the job. They have been successful as individual contributors, and if they have previously given direction to others, it has often been in the form of immediate orders or requests. They have been responsible for their own behaviors and successes but not those of subordinates. Thus, the new physician manager must not only learn the skills of delegation but also may need to adopt completely different behaviors and attitudes toward work.

This chapter addresses four aspects of delegation: why and how to delegate work to others, making delegation an inclusive process, following up, and using delegation to develop staff.

Why and How to Delegate Work to Others

The answer to "Why delegate?" may seem obvious: There is simply too much work for the manager to do alone, so it must be divided up among individuals capable of performing the tasks. But there are other reasons for delegation. Except in very simple organizations where just a small number of jobs are performed and the tasks are repetitive, work in a health care setting generally requires multiple individuals working at varying levels of complexity. No one individual, including the manager, possesses all the talent required to carry out a department's operations. The manager's job, then, is to coordinate the work of the employees and to ensure that they are achieving the right results.

For the administrator who is orienting the physician to a management role, it is important to help him or her understand everyone's role in the department or service. In addition to reviewing written job descriptions, the physician manager should "shadow" each employee during a busy time of the workday with the goal of learning what that person is responsible for and how that work interfaces with other jobs. While the shadowing experience also enables the physician manager to become acquainted with the individuals and develop a personal rapport, it should not be treated as an evaluation or a critique of the employees. When the orientation schedule is established, the message should be clearly conveyed that the new physician manager wants *only* to listen and learn.

The communication style and messages of these early interactions are important in setting a tone that fosters teamwork, respect, and a sense that "we're all in this together." Physicians in supervisory roles often do not realize how intimidating they can seem, simply because of their medical degree and their position as boss. If they begin a management job with a posture of authority and superiority, they may engender respect or fear, but they are not likely to get honest feedback or have problems brought to their attention.

Tips for administrators who orient the new physician manager to his or her role as a delegator are summarized in figure 3-1.

One key to effective delegation is frequent, straightforward discussion among parties who share a stake in the outcomes of

Figure 3-1. Orienting the Physician Manager to the Role of Delegator

Help the physician manager become a better delegator by:

- Reviewing written job descriptions for all positions in the unit
- Establishing a schedule for shadowing staff
- Communicating the "listen/learn" reason for shadowing
- Giving the physician manager feedback on approach and communication style
- Asking the staff what questions they have after the physician manager has spent time with them

their work. All aspects of delegation involve clear communication, requiring both the delegator and the individual accepting the assignment to agree on the work to be performed and the results that are expected.

It sounds simple to hand off work to another person or to give someone a written set of tasks. However, many managers, whether or not they are physicians, neglect the first and most important step of delegation: defining clearly the expected outcome of the work and explaining its importance.

In the anecdote at the beginning of this chapter, Dr. Baker describes a desired outcome, which is to reduce the waiting time for patients. However, she does not clearly describe a tangible goal of, let us say, reducing the wait time from twenty minutes to five minutes. She is reacting to an intuitive sense, or perhaps a complaint, that patients are waiting too long to be seen. This sense is apparently not shared by the clinicians, who offer argument and half-heartedly acquiesce to "do something." However, lacking a clearly defined goal and a shared understanding of its importance, Dr. Baker's project is doomed to fail from the outset.

Once the goal and importance of the work are clearly established and defined with specificity, the next step is to determine what work must be performed to achieve the goal. This step is best accomplished as a collaborative process. Carl Frost, a consultant on participative management processes, often advised: "No one knows better how to do the job or how to improve it than the individual who is in the position." It is always helpful to ask the staff what tasks they believe need to be performed to achieve the result. These suggestions should be brought into a planning process that will ultimately produce a statement of outcomes, milestones, responsibilities of staff members, and a timetable for completion.

The steps of the delegation process are summarized in figure 3-2.

Figure 3-2. The Steps of the Delegation Process

Ensure the success of the delegation process by:

- Defining the goal and its importance

- Communicating with staff and gaining buy-in

- Determining through a collaborative process the tasks that will need to be done

- Developing a plan that includes who will perform which tasks and a timetable with milestones

- Checking in regularly on progress

- Revising the plan as needed

- Celebrating success

Making Delegation an Inclusive Process

Managers must think about the scope of work and how to segment it into specific jobs on a variety of levels. Unless the manager job is in a brand new hospital or in a new service such as a hospice center that has been added to an existing facility, most newly hired or promoted managers will step into roles whose purpose has already been determined by the hospital's executives and board of directors. Therefore, few physician managers will need to design the work of the unit or department "from scratch."

However, a manager should think at the broadest possible level about the overall work of the unit even if it seems self-evident: What is the mission of the unit? What results—financial, clinical, service—are expected, and from whom? What skills are needed to produce these results? What tasks will individuals perform, and how will those tasks be organized?

These same questions should be probed even when delegating work on a singular project. In the anecdote at the beginning of this chapter, Dr. Baker can reasonably assume that the staff understand the reason that the ambulatory service exists. And she articulates a clear service goal of reducing wait times. However, she is vague about the specific results expected. There is no real plan or agreement about what work is required or what success will look like. Dr. Baker outlines tasks for the staff, but she does so in the form of mandates and without seeking input from those who best know their jobs. The staff give her reasons that her assignments will not produce the desired result: The clinicians do not want to, or feel they cannot, speed up their patient encounters; the scheduler cannot reasonably adjust schedules without data to support any course of action; and the receptionist is not able to take complaints directly to the manager. What Dr. Baker hears as resistance and judges to be staff inadequacy is actually her failure to lead a process that includes the steps outlined in figure 3-2.

Following is a hypothetical discussion from Dr. Baker's staff meeting that could have produced a better outcome.

Dr. Baker: I want to talk to all of you about my concern that patients are waiting too long to be seen by a doctor.

Staff physician: Why do you think that?

Dr. Baker: It just seems to me that the reception area is always full, and one of my former patients complained that she had to wait a long time.

Staff physician: We would have trouble shortening the time we have with patients. Maybe they are being scheduled too close to each other.

Scheduler: It has been awhile since we have evaluated the patient flow. Why don't I check out best practices with my professional association? We could also conduct a study of our patients' actual experience.

Dr. Baker: We could consider that. What would it cost? How long would it take?

Scheduler: I'll look into it and give you a proposal.

Dr. Baker: Good. Please let me know when you will have that ready. In the meantime, how should we handle any patient complaints or concerns?

Receptionist: I think we could put a suggestion box in the waiting room. Also, if we all keep notes of any concerns we hear about, we can discuss them at our weekly staff meetings. Since I prepare the agenda, I'll include it as a regular item.

Dr. Baker: That's a good idea. Then we can decide together how to respond to complaints. If something requires immediate attention, please page the department administrator. And if we can conduct a formal study at a reasonable cost and in a relatively short time frame, we can determine if we need to adjust our scheduling process. Thank you all for your cooperation.

The manager's job is to determine the priorities of the unit and to assess individuals' capabilities for performing the work. But once the manager has articulated the results that are expected, the staff should be included in deciding what tasks need to be performed and how they will be accomplished.

Following Up with Staff

Even when assigning work to a seasoned staff member whose capabilities are well known, it is important for the manager to check in with him or her on both a formal and an informal basis. Unwanted results often occur because one simply assumes that agreement has been reached about what should be done. Also, individuals get distracted by whatever immediate problems arise, and previously agreed upon work gets put aside. Any work plan should include a timetable for checking on the progress of the project.

Following up can take the form of an agenda item at regular staff meetings or at project review meetings. But informal follow-up is valuable, too. Simply dropping by someone's desk with a question—"Hi Cheryl, were you able to locate the data you were looking for?"—shows ongoing interest and reinforces the importance of the work. However, new physician managers who are accustomed to working independently rather than delegating should be careful not to micromanage. Finding the right degree of oversight is not always easy, and it must vary depending on the skills and experience of both the manager and the subordinate. That said, most problems that result from too much or too little oversight can be avoided by establishing the process for checking in at the outset of a project.

Follow-up also involves providing clarity of direction and making certain that the delegator and the person carrying out the assignment have the same expectations. For instance, queries such as these are helpful: "When you said you would have the data next month, did you mean the beginning or the end of the month?" "What kind of report are you planning? Shall we agree that a one-page written summary will be fine?"

The ultimate follow-up is the manager's declaration that a project or piece of work has been completed and the results are known. It is not uncommon for projects to drift away if the work is not going as planned or if those involved have minimal interest in it. When these issues arise, people lose their energy for work and sense their talents are not valued. Celebrating the end of a project with pizza at a staff meeting or a note that acknowledges good efforts is a way to reinforce the importance of the work. If the work is very long term in scope, one should recognize milestones along the way. Everyone needs to know what is expected of him or her and that achievement of the goal matters.

Tips for following up are summarized in figure 3-3.

Using Delegation to Develop Staff

When the manager has a specific goal in mind, it is natural for him or her to have clear ideas of what work should be

Figure 3-3. Tips for Following Up with Staff

Improve follow-up with staff members by:

- Scheduling formal check-ins
- Informally asking staff how the work is progressing
- Clarifying and reinforcing understanding about the work
- Acknowledging milestones and end points
- Celebrating success

performed and how it should be done to achieve that result. Thus, one has the tendency not only to describe the expected results but also to prescribe the methods and manner of work to be used to achieve them. While it may be hard to let go of one's ideas about how work should be carried out, the reality is that the results are often improved when a fresh set of eyes is brought to the task.

Another reason to delegate is to develop and positively motivate a staff member by entrusting him or her with bringing his or her own ideas to work processes. Experimenting, encountering trial and error, and searching for information are all aspects of learning. The opportunity to learn is an opportunity to grow, with the consequence that the employee is highly engaged in the work. The flip side of this engagement is the demoralization that occurs when the manager demonstrates a "my way or the highway" attitude or hovers over the employee, saying or implying "I would do it another way."

A frequently cited definition of management is "getting work done through other people." The most successful leaders know that their staffs feel both motivated and rewarded when given free rein to determine how to do the job. In their experience with patients or research, physicians are accustomed to controlling the way they carry out the work. Transitioning from practitioner to manager requires a shift in thinking about work as well as the assistance of a thoughtful administrator to help navigate the process.

Conclusion

A manager's failure to delegate tasks and responsibilities to staff will result in his or her being overburdened and the work product being less than optimal. But delegating is more than handing off some tasks. When a manager defines the goal of the work to be performed, seeks input from staff on what tasks will need to be performed, allows the staff freedom in how they do the work, and follows up rigorously, the goal is likely to be achieved. Even better, it will have been achieved with a more positive result because of the creative input of staff and will give a sense of satisfaction to all who helped make it happen.

4

Managing the Poor Performer

**Seek the help of advisers
and use corrective-action guidelines
to assist employees who need
to improve their performance.**

When I became a hospital vice president, I felt well prepared for the job. I had been chief of my division and had worked hand in hand with a talented administrative director who helped me learn about budgets, scheduling, facilities management, and planning. We were a great team and really enjoyed our work.

Therefore, I was taken aback when I had big problems with a long-time staff assistant I inherited with my new job. Mary Jane was very professional with me personally and seemed eager to follow my direction, but she appeared aloof from her peers; worked at her own pace; and, according to others in the department, was not a team player and spent time making personal calls. I was told that many of the staff avoided her so they "wouldn't get on her wrong side." Since these reports were secondhand and because she seemed so loyal to me, I thought it would be wrong to accuse her of anything. And even though she did not work as quickly as my former administrator, I wanted to be respectful of her long tenure with the department. In truth, I didn't want a confrontation with her and didn't know what I would tell her to do differently, anyway. It wasn't like she was making big mistakes or stealing the petty cash.

Morale in the department was not good. Talented new staff came and went. We really were not gelling as a team. It took me a long time—too long, I realize now—to see that Mary Jane was the source of much of the dissatisfaction. I also realized belatedly that others saw me as the problem. In their eyes, I was supposed to fix things; instead, I was perpetuating the difficulties.

My wife said I should just fire her; a colleague I confided in suggested that I bring in a consultant to do team building; and my former administrator urged me to speak with Mary Jane candidly and document my conversation. Ultimately, I only did the latter, and she resigned in tears. I felt bad about the way she left. But I have to say, morale in the department is much better, and I'm really glad she is gone.

---------------------Chris Carter, MD, Vice President, Clinical Services

Introduction

Author Ken Blanchard wrote: "No employee seeks to be mediocre; all seek to be magnificent."[1] The first day on a new job is generally an exciting one for both the employee and the manager who hired him or her. Both look forward to a work situation that will be rewarding and meaningful. Yet every manager has lamented at one time or another about employees whose skills, abilities, or attitudes were inadequate, and most employees can point to a supervisor in their experience who did not handle their or other employees' performance issues appropriately or successfully.

Dealing with a staff member who is not performing well is a challenge for any manager, but the task is perhaps even more difficult for new physician managers who themselves have been highly motivated and successful achievers throughout their academic and clinical experience.

This chapter addresses five aspects of managing poor performers: identifying performance issues, determining appropriate corrective actions, understanding and applying progressive discipline, resources and tools to support performance improvement, and tips for correcting performance deficiencies.

Identifying Performance Issues

Knowing whether an employee is performing poorly seems simple. One sees, of course, the results of his or her work, or the lack of results in some cases. The work may contain errors, or it may have resulted in complaints from patients, customers, or co-workers. Something is going wrong, so one can conclude there is a performance problem, correct?

Probably, but possibly not. In the case of Dr. Carter and Mary Jane, we know only his observations and actions but not those of Mary Jane. Consider how he diagnosed her performance issues. First, he compared her with his former administrative aide, and Mary Jane was deemed to be less efficient. Second, others told him that she spent time on personal matters and was somehow hurtful to people who "got on her wrong side," though he did not observe this characterization firsthand. Third, he attributed the poor morale, staff turnover, and lack of teamwork to her behaviors. He concluded he was right because the situation improved after she was gone.

For the sake of argument, consider the following possibilities: that Mary Jane was working with performance standards established by previous managers and did not know what Dr. Carter expected of her; that a co-worker of Mary Jane's, out of jealousy or resentment, fabricated the stories about her misusing time, and Mary Jane's aloofness was a way of distancing herself from the trouble; that the turnover could have been caused by other factors such as poor job design or better opportunities elsewhere; that the lack of teamwork and poor morale were a result of Dr. Carter's unwillingness to address the situation—whatever its root cause; and that morale improved because Dr. Carter finally took action and was leading with greater confidence. And of course, it is possible that Mary Jane was indeed performing below standard but that some of these other factors also contributed to the overall problems of the department.

The point is that it is not always easy to diagnose poor performance and its cause, yet it is a fundamental skill that good managers acquire. Doctors are accustomed to diagnosing illness with a process that brings together their familiarity with symptoms, their medical knowledge, their analysis of test results, and their patient's history. They would not say "I assume this patient's fever is due to the flu because it is flu season." They would conduct thorough diagnostic procedures before reaching a conclusion and prescribing treatment.

Physicians who become managers—indeed, all managers—should perform a diagnostic review with an employee who seems not to perform well. Figure 4-1 lists the questions to consider in that exercise.

Determining Appropriate Corrective Actions

Once the manager has diagnosed and clearly understands the performance problem, he or she may respond in a variety of ways. No single right answer to a performance issue exists, and no two issues are exactly alike. Indeed, what may be an appropriate correction in one circumstance may not be the best option in another, even with the same individual. However, some basic corrective actions work well to alleviate performance problems in a large variety of circumstances.

Figure 4-1. Questions for Diagnosing Problems with Employee Performance

1. What specific evidence demonstrates the problems?

2. If the quality of work is below standard, was the employee trained to do the work? Did he or she have sufficient time in which to do it? Were the instructions clear?

3. If the problems are behavioral, has there been a history of these behaviors, or is the employee suddenly acting differently? Are you aware of personal circumstances that are affecting him or her? Are co-workers interacting inappropriately with this person?

4. Does the employee's file contain documentation of this or other problems? Has he or she been counseled or disciplined for such issues in the past?

5. What does my experience tell me about the likelihood that these problems can be corrected?

6. Who in the organization could offer an opinion or advise me in this matter based on his or her expertise in dealing with these kinds of problems?

First, talk with the employee about the problem you have identified. This conversation is not to be used to "admonish," "warn," or even "counsel." Initially, it is important simply to sit down with the employee and say what you have observed. If it is tangible, such as poor writing skills, point out the errors. If it is a behavioral issue, such as being highly opinionated and negative in staff meetings, describe what you have seen and say why this behavior is problematic. Do not accuse; instead, offer statements of concern. Then ask the employee for his or her opinion about the matter. In general, the employee's response will suggest your next step.

If the employee acknowledges the problem and wants to correct it, together you can determine probable solutions. For example, a physician who directs a major hospital service talked about hiring a new administrative assistant (AA) whom he described as fantastic in every way except her writing ability. She often left out words and used awkward syntax. In a conversation with her, he learned that she is dyslexic. They agreed that she is to review drafts of her writing with another administrative assistant in the area before turning it in to him. In turn, she helps the other AA with budget issues and in managing travel. It is a win-win solution for all involved.

If the employee does not accept that your concern is a problem or deficiency that he or she should correct, listen carefully to the rationale offered. Sometimes it reflects lack of understanding of expectations. It may also suggest that the employee disagrees with your judgment or is being purely defensive. For example, you tell Martha that you found her behavior in the staff meeting to be problematic, and she replies: "What? I was just offering my opinion." In this instance, Martha does not see her behavior as you have seen it, and you need to give a more complete explanation. You might review the dialogue that occurred in the meeting to show how her comments shut down the discussion and prevented others from offering ideas.

It is equally important to talk about the behaviors you *do* want to see. The manager has a role as a teacher, and this is an an opportunity to help Martha learn how to present criticism in a positive manner. For example, you might offer this advice to her: "Instead of saying 'I think the plan is stupid,' you might have said 'I believe the plan has some gaps. It isn't clear which staff will be involved, and the timetable seems too ambitious.'" You have shown Martha a constructive way to offer her opinion without putting her down for having one.

Several aspects of this interaction are critical to correcting performance: The manager has made a statement of expected behavior or results; he has offered concrete suggestions for improvement; and he has been fair and supportive. Significantly, he has taken the time to address the matter, thereby showing its importance. There is wisdom in the old adage "What gets attention gets attended to."

Regardless of how the dialogue goes in the initial conversation about a performance problem, the manager needs to follow up soon afterward. In Martha's case, the manager might talk with her after the next staff meeting and note that her contributions were positive and helpful. If she continues to exhibit problematic behaviors, he will also need to speak with her again immediately, placing stronger emphasis on the need for correction.

Understanding and Applying Progressive Discipline

Health care organizations typically have written policies that describe a process of corrective action. The objective is to identify performance deficiencies as soon as they are evident and to see that they are corrected with the least amount of disciplinary action necessary. If the performance problems continue, the policy calls for corrective actions to become increasingly punitive, leading up to potential termination of employment.

The progression generally includes these steps: verbal counseling; informal warning; formal written warning; written final warning; suspension (in some cases); and, as a last resort, termination.

The steps of progressive discipline are more fully described in figure 4-2.

The timetable for these actions and the type of correction depend on multiple factors, including the employee's seniority and overall performance throughout his or her tenure, the

Figure 4-2. The Steps of Progressive Discipline

1. *Verbal counseling*: a conversation to describe the problem and state corrective action required.

2. *Informal warning*: a verbal reminder of the problem, noting lack of correction, and a forecast of formal disciplinary action if the problem continues uncorrected.

3. *Formal written warning*: a written statement of the problem on approved hospital forms, including a summary of verbal warnings, the corrective actions required, a timetable for improvements to be made, and a statement of potentially greater discipline if no improvement is seen. Consultation with the human resources (HR) department is required at this and all following stages.

4. *Final written warning*: again on hospital forms, a written statement of the continuation of the problem and the manager's review during the period of the warning, plus a new (generally much shorter) timetable for immediate improvement, with notice that failure to improve could result in termination.

5. *Suspension*: documented in writing, a period of days that an employee will be released from work without pay as punishment for failure to correct problems, accompanied by a warning that termination is imminent. (Note that suspension is rarely used in this way in contemporary times. If suspension is used at all, it is typically a period for investigation of a problem during which time the employee often continues to be paid.)

6. *Termination*: a statement that the employee is discharged from employment at the hospital. The statement is written on hospital forms and accompanied by documentation of actions taken by the manager and the hospital to attempt to achieve corrective action. Additional information about the employee's rights as well as pay and benefits are attached to the statement.

impact or repercussions of the performance problems, and the employee's progress in correcting the problems.

Such policies are included in a supervisor's manual and contained in employee handbooks that are issued to new hires. If health care employees are covered by a collective bargaining agreement, the contract with the union will also address the disciplinary process and ways the employee may challenge, or grieve, the supervisor's actions.

All managers and supervisors should be familiar with the policy manual and union contracts if applicable. The HR department is responsible for writing and updating policies regarding employment and for maintaining current union agreements. Once a manager believes he or she should initiate a formal disciplinary process, he or she should consult with an HR representative. It is important to know how the organization has dealt with similar issues in the past and to use the appropriate language and forms.

Furthermore, the manager must seek guidance and follow the formal protocol because the employee may challenge the disciplinary action in one of a number of ways. He or she could file a formal grievance that would call for a thorough review of the manager's decisions and actions, and if those are found faulty, the employee could be reinstated and/or have other disciplinary actions negated. Sometimes employees seek legal recourse against the organization if they disagree with the discipline. They may engage a private attorney or contact a state or federal agency such as the Equal Employment Opportunity Commission or the Office of Civil Rights to complain that the action taken by the employer was discriminatory or violated legally protected rights. These cases are often protracted, and the manager will work with HR and with the health care organization's legal counsel in defending his or her actions.

We offer a comment about summary termination: Most performance issues should be responded to with progressive corrective actions. However, some infractions are so egregious that they may warrant immediate dismissal from employment. Typically, these situations include activity such as property theft or physical violence. Even in these circumstances, it is prudent to suspend the accused employee during a period of investigation and to proceed with termination if warranted when all the facts have been accumulated and documented. In such instances, the HR department and security personnel should be consulted immediately.

Resources and Tools to Support Performance Improvement

Plainly and simply, dealing with a staff person's poor performance is not fun. Few of us enjoy sitting in judgment on another person, especially when that person is making an honest effort and is not succeeding. Yet one of a manager's most significant responsibilities is to help each subordinate be as effective in his or her work as possible, and inevitably, a time will come in the manager's experience when he or she will need to help employees correct performance deficiencies and/or to terminate them from their position.

Fortunately, many support staff and tools are available to a health care manager in this circumstance, some of which have been mentioned earlier in the chapter. The best support for a physician manager is an administrative aide who has undergone training and has experience in personnel matters. It is valuable to have another's expertise and equally valuable to have another set of eyes to examine the situation and offer objective review.

Whether or not such an assistant is available, the HR department is a critical resource for any manager dealing with performance difficulties. Not only do HR professionals know the policies and legal ramifications of situations but they also have information about cases that have set precedents and can identify other resources the manager may need, from legal advisers to performance coaches to forensic psychologists to an employee assistance program. Human resources professionals can also be called on to mediate difficult discussions, to translate policy for both the manager and the employee, and to facilitate a termination if necessary.

In addition to understanding policies and the basic aspects of employment laws, such as those regarding fair hiring and firing, managers will benefit from special courses in conflict resolution, performance management, and communications. These classes are available through local colleges, professional seminars, and often through the training and development programs offered by staff within the organization.

Tips for Correcting Performance Deficiencies

In dealing with poor performers, the manager should keep the following tips in mind:

- Tackle performance problems at the earliest possible opportunity. Contrary to wishful thinking, they do not go away by themselves.
- Remember that the best solutions are those reached mutually at the local level. Give the employee a fair opportunity to correct any problems.
- Revisit your own expectations. Are the performance standards clear and fair? Have they been communicated adequately?
- Use your administrative aide as a sounding board and seek his or her advice.
- Know the relevant supervisory policies or where to access them.
- Consult HR professionals before starting a formal disciplinary process.
- Do not be intimidated by the possibility of legal actions, discrimination charges, or grievances. If you deal with employ

ees fairly and seek appropriate advice, you will generally prevail in the event of challenges to your actions.

■ Remember that performance management is an aspect of your job that you perform every day, not just when problems arise. Ongoing dialogue about how to achieve results is the best way to ensure they are attained.

We close this section with tips for managing poor performance of the brand new employee and the long-service employee.

Managing New Employees' Poor Performance

Many health care organizations define the first three or six months of employment as a probationary period for new hires. It is a common but incorrect assumption that an employee can be terminated during that time without cause. The probationary period is established as a time for explicit review of how expectations are being met by both the manager and the employee, requiring a deliberate declaration of the probability of future success. If problems are identified, they can, one hopes, be resolved at the beginning of the employment tenure. While it is true that less documentation is needed to support a termination during an employee's probationary period, the employee must still be given a fair chance to correct problems, and any performance issues must be documented. A termination that appears whimsical can leave the employer vulnerable to charges of discrimination.

Managing Long-Service Employees' Poor Performance

Long-service employees are sometimes thought to be "off limits" in terms of correcting their performance problems. The assumption is that poor behaviors and substandard work have been tolerated for so long that it would be unfair to address these issues late in an employee's career. The reality is that it is never too late to correct performance problems, and it remains an abiding obligation of the manager to do so. It would be wrong to simply change the standards of what is acceptable and discipline the employee for past mistakes. But it is perfectly appropriate to acknowledge that new expectations are being established and that the employee will have both time and support to achieve results under the new standard. It is important to treat all employees in the same job classification alike.

When staff are rewarded only for service and not for performance, everyone involved in the situation suffers. Whether Mary Jane was or was not the source of her organization's difficulties, the manager's reluctance to deal with issues involving her performance and her relationship with co-workers contributed to the poor morale of the department. Dr. Carter was correct in one sense: He was the problem.

Conclusion

When a staff member is not performing well, the manager must first understand the reasons for the poor performance and then work diligently to help the employee correct any deficiencies. If factors beyond the employee's control, such as lack of clear direction or inadequate support from colleagues, are part of the problem, they must be dealt with before the employee is expected to improve. If an individual's poor performance is not corrected, the manager must take appropriate but decisive steps toward termination. Dealing with a poor performer is one of the least enjoyable but most necessary jobs of the manager. The morale and productivity of all the staff depend on it.

Reference

1. Ken Blanchard, "Foreword," in *1001 Ways to Reward Employees*, by Bob Nelson (New York: Workman, 2005).

5

Managing the Successful Performer

Do not take high achievers
for granted. Retain your top talent
by motivating, evaluating,
and rewarding them.

Marlene Rathbun, administrative director in Dr. Grant Kirk's department, came to see me today, and it was a troubling discussion. As vice president for the specialty units, I'm responsible for Dr. Kirk's department and a number of others. I've always held both Marlene and Dr. Kirk in the highest esteem and have used them as a model for how to run a great unit as well as an ideal partnership of a physician and an operations person.

I'm concerned because Marlene is planning to resign. She says that while Dr. Kirk gives her a great deal of latitude in decisions around such matters as budget, staffing, and scheduling, he never praises her or tells her what she could do better. When she asks him for feedback, he makes remarks like "You know I think you are doing a great job." Or he jokes about sending her more problems.

She says she accepts him for who he is, and the lack of communication is not a big deal, but she is feeling dead-ended and is not learning anything new. Although torn because of her loyalty to Dr. Kirk and the hospital, she says she needs to think about her future. I asked her why she came to see me. Was it because she wants me to talk her out of it or try to get her a pay increase? She said no, that it was just a courtesy visit so that I wouldn't be caught off guard.

I thanked her, and she left the office. But I can't help wondering if she really does want me to do something to stop her. On the other hand, she's a mature adult and knows what she wants in her life. Maybe it is time for her to move on. I just know this is going to be a big blow for Grant Kirk and the staff in that department.

---------------------------------Carol Oakwood, MD, Vice President

Introduction

All employers are gratified when staff produce the right results and contribute to the positive environment of the organization. Furthermore, it is reasonable that leaders expect employees to do so. Yet folklore suggests that managers spend 80 percent of their time dealing with the 20 percent of the workforce who are less productive or otherwise problematic. Busy administrators often take competent employees for granted, assuming they know they are doing a good job and, because they are not complaining, are satisfied in their position. These assumptions are made at the peril of the organization. Talented employees have or will find other work options. Without praise from their manager, recognition from the organization, and opportunities for growth or development, such employees will seek other opportunities, leaving a gap that is both expensive and difficult to fill.

This chapter addresses five aspects of managing the successful employee: recognizing and nurturing good performance, maximizing the formal evaluation process, mentoring and developing subordinates for promotion, resources available to help sustain great performance, and tips for making the successful employee more successful.

Recognizing and Nurturing Good Performance

What is good performance? While an amount of subjectivity is expected in the response, most managers talk about results. Job descriptions specify the work to be done, and performance plans should indicate what results are expected and a timetable for achieving them. The best performance plans are developed as a kind of "contract" between the manager and the employee that gives them an opportunity to check in along the way and talk about how things are going. When an employee is doing well, these check-ins are moments for the manager to praise and reinforce the employee's work. The more complex and long term the work, the more important it is to have milestones to celebrate progress and keep the employee motivated.

The performance of managers is difficult to quantify and measure. Because their results are achieved through other people, success correlates with their ability to direct their subordinates' work. They are judged, both formally and informally, on the overall accomplishments of an entire unit or department. Their achievements are not often celebrated because even as goals are reached on one project, several others loom large. Momentary successes get lost amid the array of problems to be solved. While effective managers will both privately and publicly acknowledge their subordinates' results, they avoid taking credit themselves. This does not mean, however, that they should not be praised. Senior leaders must ensure that managers at every level are shown appreciation, just as they themselves should expect it from the board of directors.

In the case of Marlene Rathbun, one can see that she is a good performer in the eyes of her employer. She is cited as a role model and a significant part of the department's success. Yet she is unhappy and "burned out." Clearly her supervisor has provided little overt praise or acknowledgment. And while she perhaps hints that such recognition might reverse her decision to leave, Marlene likely has reached the maximum potential in that role and will be more fulfilled in a new job.

What is sad about this situation is that Marlene's dissatisfaction was allowed to fester and grow to the point where she determined her only recourse was to leave her job. Before one is too critical of Dr. Kirk, however, one should ask whether the organization ever told him he was required to evaluate his staff or gave him the tools to do so. Also, could Marlene have been more forthcoming about her interests and needs? If Dr. Kirk were not responsive, could she not have talked to Dr. Oakwood when an opportunity was still available to expand her job responsibilities or explore other options?

Sometimes the "right" answer is indeed for an individual to voluntarily leave a good work experience to find an even better one. But in reality, too many good employees grow disenchanted with their work because they lack positive support from their managers and are offered no plan by which to further develop within his or her current job or within the organization more broadly.

The best way to ensure that good performance is recognized and nurtured is to establish formal processes for doing so. Following are the components of that process:

- A written job description that states the purpose of the role and the results expected, in broad terms
- A written performance plan—a kind of understood "contract"—developed annually by the manager and subordinate together outlining goals and timetables for expected results
- Regular meetings (weekly, biweekly, or monthly) to review progress, talk about difficulties, and thank each other
- Annual performance reviews that include a written self-review by the subordinate and written comments by the manager
- Regularly scheduled project review meetings for the relevant team members to review progress, talk about difficulties, and celebrate milestone successes
- A formal reward and recognition program that encourages employees to acknowledge each others' performance and that gives the organization an opportunity to celebrate the behaviors and achievements it wants to reinforce

Maximizing the Formal Evaluation Process

Most health care organizations use some method of performance review. Typically, the manager reviews each direct report on an annual basis using a form or process that is promulgated by the human resources (HR) department and endorsed by senior management. The objective, of course, is to ensure that employees are given feedback about what aspects of the job they are doing well and in what areas they can improve. The concept is widely accepted as a basic component of leadership by authors of management texts, including this one.

Perhaps one reason the topic is frequently presented as an educational issue is that reviews are so often conducted badly. The performance review meeting can be an awkward and uncomfortable experience for both manager and employee, and in many cases, both individuals are glad to find excuses to bypass it altogether. The review is made more difficult and stressful when the manager is expected to discuss a salary increase related to the year's performance.

Several reasons can be cited to explain the fear, distaste, and avoidance this highly endorsed process receives. A common one is that the manager has failed to address a performance issue with the employee all year and now feels he or she must do so but is embarrassed to address it so long after its initial occurrence. Another reason is that the meeting is treated as a recitation of activities rather than a discussion of capabilities, skills to be learned, desired achievements, and career planning. Thus, it is seen as meaningless to both parties.

Managers are uncomfortable talking about salary because they do not fully understand how the pay increase policy they have been instructed to deliver correlates with the performance they are discussing. Inevitably, employees react to the manager's discomfort with a suspicion that they are not being treated equitably or that their good work has not been fully recognized with appropriate compensation.

Physicians in management roles are even more discomfited than most by the process. Many have had no training in performance management. Their experience in evaluating others has been related to clinical performance in accordance with methods they have studied throughout their professional training as doctors. Tools such as job descriptions and performance-rating instruments are alien documents. In the past, their own salaries were a function of a schedule that pays interns and residents a specific salary based on years in training and specialty. Beyond their residencies, physicians negotiated pay with the chief of their service. If the physician was a key administrator, the salary was negotiated with the organization's president or board. Additionally, as previously noted, physicians become successful through their mastery of a body of medical knowledge, their ability to conduct scientific research, and their ability to transfer their learning to the practice of treating patients. It is no wonder that they are bewildered and put off by an evaluation form that may look at every aspect of a job, from attendance and punctuality to ability to deal with change and interpersonal relationships.

So how does one make the formal review process a worthwhile experience that advances both the organization's goals and the employee's career aspirations? Following are keys to making performance management successful:

- Recognizing that managing performance is not a once-per-year meeting but a year-round activity that includes ongoing discussion of agreed-upon performance standards and progress toward goals
- Learning, through formal classes or mentoring, how to talk about performance difficulties and set a course of corrective action
- Acknowledging good performance on a regular basis, individually and in front of peers
- Having the employee prepare a written self-review prior to the evaluation meeting
- Separating pay discussions from performance reviews, even when a relationship exists between the two
- Working with HR to ensure an understanding of the forms, terminology, and pay policy

When performance management has been an ongoing activity, not only is the annual review not onerous, it is a pleasant and productive experience. The components of a successful performance review are shown in figure 5-1.

Mentoring and Developing Subordinates for Promotion

Employers are pleased when they hear their staff make comments such as "I love my job" or "I can't imagine working anywhere else." But good managers learn that job satisfaction is not self-sustaining. It must be regularly nurtured. Also, satisfaction has a different meaning to different employees and may even carry a different meaning for the same employee when circumstances change. Satisfaction typically increases when an employee's desire for new challenges or increased responsibility is realized.

In much the same way that parents take pride in their children's successes, many managers say they feel most fulfilled in their work when they see staff whom they have developed move up in the organization or move on to more senior roles elsewhere. However, the gratification that comes with others' successes evolves over time as managers themselves grow in their leadership roles.

Figure 5-1. Components of a Performance Review Meeting

Conduct a successful performance review by:

- Reflecting on the past year: Were expectations met? What prevented goals from being met?
- Noting highlights: What were the greatest achievements, advances, and/or learning areas?
- Planning for next year: What activities or behaviors need to be continued, stopped, or changed?
- Discussing the employee's career aspirations and how the manager can help him or her accomplish personal goals
- Thanking each other for mutual support

Consider the reason one is first appointed to a management position. Typically, the individual has been tapped for the job because he or she has been a stellar achiever in an individual capacity and has demonstrated some characteristics of leadership, such as sound decision making, strong interpersonal skills, and commitment to organizational values and goals. However, he or she has only been responsible for his or her own behaviors and results, not for those of others. For new physician managers particularly, having conquered the challenges of medical school, residency, and research or clinical practice, the notion of subordinating one's own achievements to those of others is indeed an alien concept.

What happens in the transformation from individual achiever to manager whose main accomplishment is the success of others? Several steps are necessary for this shift to occur, including the following:

- The new manager's supervisor must define the job and the results expected to be achieved by the unit for which the new manager is responsible.
- If not already developed, an organization chart needs to be drawn that graphically displays the functions of the unit and how they relate to one another.
- As mentioned earlier, job descriptions and individual business plans should be constructed for each job and modified for the individual based on skills and experience.
- The manager must prepare meeting and review schedules to establish a plan for tracking both individual and group performance.
- Milestones should be acknowledged, with interim successes celebrated and plan revisions made as necessary.

With these steps achieved, the new manager has a framework for delegating work and monitoring results. But this sounds like bureaucracy, not accomplishment. How does this process translate into success for the manager and development for the employee?

The simple answer is that with practice and experience in following these steps, managers hone the skill of developing a high-functioning organization with clearly defined roles and goals. Meeting objectives through collaboration and teamwork and then raising the bar and achieving even greater goals bring a sense of victory and the promise of continuing success. The manager's personal accomplishment is gained with the recognition that such wins are not possible without giving staff the tools and inspiration to do the job and providing the structure for the team to work together.

The steps in transforming from individual achiever to manager listed earlier create the foundation for the unit to achieve results and help the manager consider what each subordinate needs to deliver. Additional effort on the manager's part is required to help each individual maximize his or her potential. In the earlier description of an effective performance review meeting, the manager was urged to discuss the employee's career aspirations and needed skill development in addition to the work itself.

A good way to begin this conversation is to have the employee prepare a written self-review prior to meeting to discuss performance. In addition to establishing a framework on which to build goals, the self-review form also gives the employee an idea of the agenda you will follow, making the meeting itself less intimidating. Figure 5-2 lists some sample questions to include on a self-review form.

After these topics are discussed, the manager should prepare a written follow-up that reflects agreements on accomplishments; plans for the next year; and commitments to training, development, and support. Needed corrective actions must be included in addition to praise and encouragement. It should go without saying that the tone of both the meeting and the written document should convey the manager's sincere commitment to helping the employee be successful and satisfied in his or her job.

Figure 5-2. Self-Review Questions

1. What have been your greatest accomplishments during the past year?
2. What have you not achieved that you had planned to? Is it still worth doing?
3. Which parts of your job are most satisfying? Which are least satisfying?
4. What are your major objectives for next year?
5. What would you like to learn more about? What can you teach others?
6. How do I best support you in your work? What else could I do to be helpful to you?

Resources Available to Help Sustain Great Performance

Once one recognizes that performance management is a skill to be learned and practiced over time if it is to be mastered, many resources and tools are available to support this effort.

Resources include the following:

- Educational courses available at area colleges
- Professional seminars offered by the Center for Creative Leadership, the American Hospital Association, the American Management Association, and many other organizations
- Books and journal articles
- Training programs offered by the hospital
- Executive coaching
- Employee relations and organization development staff in human resources

Among the variety of tools available are the following:

- Performance appraisal forms and systems, ranging from simple checklists to an elaborate 360-degree evaluation process that includes feedback from peers, customers, and managers
- Self-evaluation forms

- Employee satisfaction surveys, both informal and formal
- Reward and recognition programs, which may range from printed thank you cards distributed by co-workers to gift and certificate programs to organization-wide ceremonies in which hospital leaders present plaques or trophies to individuals and teams who have been selected by their peers as examples of stellar performance
- "Lunch with the boss" as a way to thank individual employees, or pizza at staff meetings to acknowledge the team's effort

All these tools and resources are valuable and should be used when appropriate, but one need not be overwhelmed by them. By starting with a commitment to provide regular feedback, to bring empathy to conversations about performance, and to thank staff genuinely and frequently, a new manager is already developing the skills to appraise performance and keep one's best employees motivated and satisfied.

Tips for Making the Successful Employee More Successful

At a large, male-dominated research laboratory in the East, when the HR department was introducing a formal reward and recognition program for the employees of the facility, the laboratory leader reportedly scoffed at the initiative, saying "Our motto here is that real men don't need praise." That macho viewpoint implied that individuals should be expected to perform well without positive feedback and that self-satisfaction is enough to reward good performance. Happily, that attitude was ignored, and several years later, the laboratory continues to generate many nominations for individual and team awards, and its celebrations are elaborate and joyous.

There is an old saying that "when you give people crumbs, they will give you back loaves." Indeed, a little praise from a manager goes a long way toward motivating an employee to continue to work hard and deliver results. Inexperienced managers sometimes believe that if an employee receives a great amount of positive reinforcement, he or she will not hear or accept negative feedback when problems occur. In reality, employees who are accustomed to being told they are succeeding will work even harder to correct problems in order to restore the confidence of their manager.

Figure 5-3 provides tips for making the successful employee even more successful.

Conclusion

It is a true joy to work with talented staff who produce great results. Managers depend on their successful employees to accomplish the goals of the unit and also to mentor and inspire others. It is important to remember that the high achievers need feedback and nurturing as much as do poor performers. Through acknowledging and rewarding employees' accomplishments, individual and team morale is kept high.

Experienced managers learn that their own success is realized through the achievements of those whom they direct.

Figure 5-3. Making a Successful Employee More Successful

Keep the high achiever sharp and engaged by:

- Taking the performance appraisal process seriously and making it a priority
- Raising the bar when the employee has mastered a new challenge
- Discussing the employee's career aspirations and educational interests
- Making it safe to discuss job opportunities outside your department or hospital
- Asking the employee to mentor and teach other staff
- Documenting the employee's achievements and acknowledging them in front of his or her peers
- Letting your manager know about your stellar employees so that success travels upward

6

Firing:
When and How to Do It

**When absolutely necessary, terminate
employees whose performance or behavior
does not meet organizational standards.
But do it legally and fairly, preserving
the individual's dignity.**

I hired Carl as the office manager after a lengthy search. The previous manager, Millie, had been much beloved by staff, physicians, and patients and had run the office with the precision of a Swiss watch. It seemed everyone in the hospital came to her retirement party. I knew she would be hard to replace, so I tried to be very thorough. No candidate emerged that seemed exactly right, and as time went on, I, along with everyone else, was growing anxious. Carl was a compromise choice. He had much of the right experience in that he had managed an office, but it was a much smaller office with an insurance company. I had hoped to find someone with a health care background but felt his skills would be transferable.

When the receptionists first complained about Carl, I dismissed their criticism as an unfair comparison to Millie. He was attempting to introduce efficiency measures that he had used in his former job, and the receptionists balked at having to fill out forms and track the time spent on certain tasks like photocopying. Then I started getting complaints from the nurses and doctors. The supplies were inadequate or wrong and the schedules were confused. The accounting department and patients were not getting information they needed in a timely way.

Of course I discussed these issues with Carl at our weekly meetings. He agreed that there were difficulties but thought he was making headway with the staff and learning how the hospital works. My personal concern about Carl was that he was always in his office on the computer. But I chided myself for being like others and comparing him to Millie, who had been such a presence in the reception area. So I mentioned it, but when he responded that he was working on systems issues, I let it go.

After six months, when morale was at a low ebb, the unit was disorganized, and Carl still had not gained the confidence of anyone in the department, I called him into my office and told him that it wasn't working out and that I thought he would have to leave. He was quite upset and said this really caught him off guard. He pleaded with me to give him more time. He said he was having some problems at home, that he really needed this job, and that he would try harder.

Even though I truly doubt that he can be successful, I am tempted to give him another six months. I want to be fair to the guy, and I also don't have a better alternative right now. Maybe I'll start a quiet search for a replacement and then let him go.

-------------------------------- Sylvia McIntosh, MD, Chief, Urology

Introduction

Deciding when someone's performance warrants termination and conducting the discharge in the most appropriate way are among the most difficult tasks a manager must perform. Because firings are thankfully infrequent, even the most experienced managers sometimes shy away from this action or perform it in a clumsy manner that wounds not only the terminated employee but his or her co-workers as well. Despite the distasteful aspect of removing a person from employment, it is sometimes the best course of action. As Peter Drucker said, "Executives owe it to the organization and to their fellow workers not to tolerate nonperforming individuals in important jobs."[1]

This chapter addresses four topics related to involuntary termination: recognizing when firing is the best course of action, actions to take prior to termination, available resources for the manager and employee in this circumstance, and tips for handling a termination effectively.

Recognizing When Firing Is the Best Course of Action

There are times when a termination is the clear resolution to a workplace situation. Supervisory policy manuals and employee handbooks usually spell out infractions that will result in dismissal. Among those most typically noted are abuse of a patient or co-worker, theft, malicious destruction of property, reporting to work under the influence of drugs or alcohol, possession of weapons, and gross insubordination. Though usually preceded by an investigation to determine whether mitigating circumstances are at play or prior warnings have been given, firing an employee for these severe violations of policy is readily understood.

Managers are less certain about whether or when to terminate employees whose job performance is not meeting standards. And they are even more at a loss when the issues are behavioral, such as an employee not getting along with co-workers or having emotional or physical problems that affect the quality of work.

Should Dr. McIntosh fire Carl after six months of job performance that has not met expectations? It is clear that Carl is not succeeding. He has not gained the confidence of his subordinates, colleagues, or even Dr. McIntosh, who hired him. He does not appear to have adapted to the culture of the hospital and may be retreating to his office rather than dealing with problems in the unit. Following a highly popular employee like Millie, Carl began his employment facing a tough transition. Though Dr. McIntosh has met with him regularly, she may not have provided sufficient orientation or resources to help him do the job better. Nonetheless, the results at this juncture are unsatisfactory, and Dr. McIntosh appropriately recognizes that some action needs to be taken, though whether it should be an immediate termination is questionable.

Terminations carry serious consequences for both the employee who is fired and the organization. In determining whether performance difficulties warrant termination, the manager should carefully consider the questions posed in figure 6-1.

By answering the questions in figure 6-1, a manager can recognize that a termination for substandard performance is indeed appropriate when and if the employee has been given ample time to understand the job and expectations, resources and training (for skills not required prior to hire), and appropriate notice that failure to improve would result in termination. If these conditions have not been met, the manager will need to take a number of actions before terminating an employee.

Actions to Take Prior to Termination

Firing can mean the loss of one's livelihood, cause damage to an individual's self-esteem, and shake the confidence of others

Figure 6-1. Considerations in Determining Whether to Terminate an Employee

1. Does the employee understand the job and what is expected of him or her? What evidence indicates that he or she does or does not understand?

2. Has the employee been given sufficient time to learn and be proficient at the job? If not, how much more time would be needed?

3. Does the employee have the requisite skills? Which ones are lacking? Can they be learned quickly and well enough for the employee to succeed?

4. Has the employee shown improvement following counseling or other corrective action?

5. Does the employee know that failure to improve can result in termination? When and how was he or she informed?

6. What are the consequences if this employee is terminated? Who will do the work? How will co-workers react? Will the termination be challenged?

in the workforce. It should be a last resort after all *appropriate* actions have been taken to help the employee succeed. An equal level of destruction can occur if an employee is allowed to stay on the job when he or she is failing. Competent employees grow weary of picking up the slack, resent the failing employee, and lose confidence in the manager who is not taking action to correct the situation. A successful termination should result in the terminated employee leaving with dignity intact, understanding that he or she is not in the right job. It should also be done in a way that others perceive as fair.

Therefore, the actions leading up to the termination are critical. In chapter 4, "Managing the Poor Performer," the manager is cautioned to consult with the human resources (HR) department once the corrective actions become formal. At the point when an employee is told in writing that failure to improve could result in termination, the manager should no longer "fly solo" in the ensuing process. Terminations have great personal, financial, and organizational consequences, and the manager needs to understand and plan for them. The conversations with HR should occur before warnings are put in writing and at each stage of progressive discipline that follows (see chapter 4).

Throughout the course of corrective action, the manager should be talking with the employee about the specific results expected and why they are not being achieved. At established checkpoints, if sufficient improvement has not been made, both the employee and the manager must acknowledge that deficiencies continue. If these conversations are conducted in a professional but supportive manner, the employee will realize long before he or she is terminated that the process is heading toward that potential end.

A physician who has directed a large hospital department for many years stated: "I have never fired anybody. They always fire themselves." He is a master at helping employees see their strengths and weaknesses, and he is not timid about pointing out errors and problems. While some individuals have left his office in tears, most return with a plan to show him that they can do better. And he gives them a chance to do that. Sometimes they submit their resignation. Over the years, he has had to terminate both physicians and administrative personnel, or "let them fire themselves." Yet he continues to hear from many of those same people, who seek his advice or just stay in touch. Though he is skilled in his ability to confront problems with both directness and supportiveness, he is quick to say he has both the department's administrative director and the HR department "on speed dial."

Sylvia McIntosh and Carl might both have benefited if Dr. McIntosh had taken more appropriate actions during Carl's first six months on the job. Carl shows all the signs of being in over his head. Though he had prior management experience, he relied on techniques that worked in his former job and did not adapt to the culture of the hospital. While Dr. McIntosh met with him and talked about the problems, she did not let him know his job was on the line or establish a timetable for reviewing improvement.

At the conclusion of the anecdote, she is considering giving him another six months on the job, which would be a serious mistake. She is not doing it because she sees that he will improve with time but rather out of sympathy for him and convenience for herself in finding a replacement.

An abrupt dismissal would also be wrong because she has not taken the appropriate actions to support a termination. While Dr. McIntosh should have consulted HR as soon as she began to see repeated problems and lack of improvement, it is not too late for her to seek advice and counsel now rather than simply extend his employment. She need not rescind her judgment about "things not working out," but she must demonstrate to him why he is not succeeding. She should give him a written document that explains that fairly dramatic improvement is necessary within a short time frame, say thirty days, and ask him to produce an action plan. The message should also be explicit that he will be terminated unless significant and sustainable results are achieved. Because Carl has not been able to perform adequately in the previous six months, he should probably anticipate that the likely outcome of this thirty-day "probation" will be his termination. One hopes he will seek assistance or begin looking for another job. While she needs to give him a fair chance to turn his performance around, Dr. McIntosh, in consultation with HR, should simultaneously start planning how to support his exit in terms of pay, benefits, and announcement to the community, as well as how to fill his job after he leaves.

When employees allege that their performance failures are caused by emotional or physical problems, the manager faces a number of complicated issues and should seek immediate guidance from HR and possibly from the hospital's legal counsel. These conditions may be considered disabilities, in which case the employee is afforded certain rights and protections under the law. The federal Family and Medical Leave Act provides for time off from work for the employee to take care of personal or family problems and guarantees that his or her job will not be lost. Other laws, both federal and state, protect employees from actions that would be interpreted as discrimination against them due to their disabilities. A unit manager cannot reasonably be expected to know and interpret these laws, so consulting with experts is critical.

Having said that, it is also important that a manager be able to confront performance issues, regardless of the reasons for the difficulties. The manager's job is to see that employees are producing results and, if satisfactory results are not being seen, to address the situation directly.

One physician manager confided that she suspected one of her employees was an alcoholic because he was often absent from or late to work, slurred his speech, and "smelled funny." When she was asked whether she had confronted him, the physician manager replied: "No, I didn't think I could. Isn't that against the law?" She was then asked what she would do if she saw an employee fall down and break his leg. Would she ignore the person writhing in pain in front of her? Her quick answer was that, of course, she would not; she would immediately try to help him. The physician was advised that this employee needed help as well, or at least attention. Her job is not to diagnose the problem but to talk to the employee about the behaviors she observed and the issues with his performance. Depending on his response, she could direct him to places for help, such as a confidential employee assistance program (EAP). If he denied having a problem, she must nonetheless confront the performance issues and take corrective action.

Alcoholism and a host of other physical and emotional issues can indeed be classified as disabilities, and in such cases, the manager should support the employee in finding resources that will help him or her address and conquer the problem. At the same time, the manager must not lower performance standards or excuse the employee from meeting them. The employee may need a leave of absence or some other accommodation to deal with the issues, but if he or she remains on the job, performance must be maintained.

The manager must balance being compassionate toward the ailing employee with continuing to hold him or her accountable for results. Physicians are healers, and their instincts and training may compel them to delve into the employee's health issue. But if the physician is the employee's manager, he or she must resist being the employee's doctor and remember that his or her job is to direct an effective department. Patients, hospital leaders, and other employees in the department are depending on that leadership; thus, the manager must assist the employee by appropriate referral and by using the resources available to help address such circumstances.

Available Resources for the Manager and the Employee

When an employee is fired, he or she loses employment with the hospital, not just with the immediate manager who may have delivered the news. Therefore, managers must conduct disciplinary actions and terminations in accordance with hospital policies and established procedures. As mentioned earlier, the HR department maintains policies regarding employment. Human resources personnel will also determine whether other expertise, such as legal services, is needed to advise in any given situation.

Though HR may serve a triage function to help the employee and manager obtain the support needed, one should be aware of the many resources that exist for both. Following are resources typically available within a hospital:

- Employee health services
- The hospital's contracted EAP
- Employee relations specialists in HR
- Legal services
- Employee benefits specialists in HR
- Hospital chaplains
- The supervisory policy manual
- The employee handbook
- Training programs or professional seminars

Tips for Handling a Termination Effectively

If you as a manager must fire an employee, remember the following points:

- The employee is not a failure as a person, but he or she is failing at this job.
- Your job is to manage performance and ensure results, not diagnose or solve the employee's personal problems.
- Avoiding the termination of a poor performer will result in your best performers leaving and the unit becoming demoralized.
- Do not fly solo; seek the help of HR, and use other resources.

- Expect to feel miserable; the act of terminating an employee is an implicit acknowledgment of hopes dashed and expectations thwarted—both yours and those of the employee.

If you are an administrator advising the physician manager who must fire an employee, take the following steps:

- Identify the relevant policies, and help explain them.
- Review the manager's actions that preceded the termination decision; advise on further corrective action if needed.
- Direct the manager to the appropriate professional staff in HR.
- Assist the manager in completing the correct forms and planning the termination process.
- Attend the termination meeting with the manager and be supportive of his or her actions, but also be available to the employee to assist with the logistics of departure (final paycheck, keys and identification badge, uniforms, etc.).

Conclusion

Firing an employee is perhaps the toughest job a manager must perform. In this situation, both the employee and the manager may feel he or she has failed. The best managers have acquired the skill of supporting an employee through difficult times when he or she is not succeeding while simultaneously leading him or her to a graceful exit. The desired result is that the employee leaves with dignity intact to find a more suitable position and the rest of the staff feel that the manager has acted fairly and in the best interest of the hospital.

Reference

1. Peter Drucker, "What Makes an Effective Executive," *Harvard Business Review* (June 2004): 4.

7

Dealing with Conflict

Understand the nature of conflict, techniques for dealing with it, and how to facilitate win-win solutions.

I didn't hear it myself, but I was told that the shouting between Ed and Margaret in the staff lounge could be heard in offices at the other end of the corridor. I knew there had been tension between them, but I was surprised that these two professionals would let it come to this. Ed is our financial manager, and Margaret is in charge of our computer systems. They are both competent, and I get along well with them individually. Apparently the altercation occurred when Ed accused Margaret of hiring IT [information technology] consultants who were changing the financial reports without his involvement. She allegedly retorted that his reporting methods were cumbersome and costly and that he needed to get in the new century. Since they both report directly to me, I knew I needed to deal with the situation right away.

I talked to Margaret first. She apologized for losing her temper but said that Ed was driving her crazy and making her job twice as hard as it needed to be. Her earlier attempts to get him to focus on technical improvements had failed, so she felt she needed to go forward without him. She pleaded with me to get him to accept her leadership on systems issues and respect her expertise.

When I went to see Ed afterward, he waved a letter of resignation at me. "Either she goes or I go," he said. "I have kept the department in the black for twelve years using the methods I developed myself. Everyone else in the hospital likes the work I do. If you are going to let Margaret make decisions for my area, then you don't need me here."

I told Ed, as I had told Margaret, that I was disappointed in their behavior and that I needed to think about what to do about it. The eyes of all the staff were on me as I walked back to my office.

I guess I need to document this somehow, but I don't want to make it a bigger deal than it already is. I am tempted to tell each of them just to grow up and treat each other civilly. This will blow over. It always does.

------------------ Martin Klingman, MD, Division Chief, Hematology

Introduction

Rodney King, the victim of a notorious videotaped beating by policemen that sparked riots throughout Los Angeles, pleaded "Why can't we all just get along?" Conflict is uncomfortable for most people, even those engaged in it. Whether on the street or in an office setting, one tends to walk away from confrontation or to pretend to be unaware of it. While perhaps wishing that disputes would simply resolve themselves, managers must deal with them when they occur among their staff or between staff and patients. Responsibility for performance and positive morale includes taking the necessary and often difficult steps to ensure that conflicts are resolved in appropriate and timely ways.

This chapter focuses on four aspects of conflict resolution: understanding and investigating conflicts, methods of conflict resolution, managing the effects of conflict on others, and resources available to assist in dispute resolution.

Understanding and Investigating Conflicts

Physical assaults or heated verbal arguments such as the one between Ed and Margaret usually get the attention of the manager immediately. In some situations security personnel and the human resources (HR) department are involved as well. Less visible conflicts may take place over the phone, in e-mail exchanges, or outside the work setting. Even more subtle conflicts are acted out through shunning a co-worker or using disparaging body language or gestures. Whether the conflict is "in your face" or much less observable, the manager is obligated to investigate it and see that it is resolved.

Physicians and others promoted to management roles are usually genial people with strong interpersonal skills, as these traits are sought by recruiters and search committees in identifying managerial talent. Because they work well with many different types of people themselves, these managers often assume that other adults will act maturely and settle any differences in a civil way. Therefore, they may wait to let situations resolve themselves rather than intervene.

In general, physicians have a more directive leadership style and thus are more impatient with conflict, particularly when they see it as petty and personal. They may seek immediate resolution through some form of mandate rather than engage in a process of investigation and facilitated negotiation. Advisers to physician managers need to coach them through the stages of successful conflict resolution.

In addition to having a natural tendency to avoid confrontation, managers may also be reluctant to intervene in conflicts between co-workers if they sense that their involvement might escalate the problem. They just want peace and harmony to come about, whether they believe the old adage that time heals all wounds or simply find the whole situation baffling and distasteful.

However, conflict that is allowed to fester does not resolve itself; instead, the problems compound. The combatants grow more entrenched in their positions, and co-workers feel compelled to take sides or keep a wide distance between themselves and those in conflict. Morale suffers; it becomes more difficult for teams to work together, and celebrations feel forced and uncomfortable. Ultimately the department does not achieve the best results, and talented staff leave to work in more positive environments. Thus, it is imperative that managers address conflict as soon as they are aware of it.

The manager must be a neutral party throughout the conflict resolution process. The first step in managing conflict is to investigate it. There are always at least two individuals involved; one may be a perpetrator and the other a victim, or the two may have equal leverage. In this first step, the manager meets separately with both individuals and asks them to describe what they are experiencing, what interactions they have had with each other, the duration of the conflict, and what steps they have taken to resolve it. The manager may request supporting documentation such as e-mails or meeting notes.

The types of questions that would be asked in an investigatory meeting are noted in figure 7-1.

Note that the emphasis of the questions posted in figure 7-1 is on the actions that have been taken by the parties involved to cause the problem and the actions they will need to take to resolve it. In Dr. Klingman's meetings with Margaret and Ed, he learned the nature of the conflict, but both of them put it in his lap to solve. Each felt wronged by the other and looked to Dr. Klingman to take his or her side and correct the other individual. It is no wonder he feels some frustration about the situation.

Figure 7-1. Questions for Investigating a Conflict

---

1. What is the disagreement about?
2. What action or activity caused the conflict to come about?
3. Describe your interactions with the other person.
4. How long has this conflict been going on?
5. What steps have you taken to resolve the conflict?
6. What actions would you like to see the other person take?
7. What actions do you think you should take?
8. How do you want this situation to be resolved?

Methods of Conflict Resolution

How one helps individuals resolve conflicts depends on a number of factors. Following are some questions a manager may ask before determining what approach to take:

- Is the conflict a single disagreement over a specific issue, or is there a long history of the parties not getting along with each other?
- Are multiple staff members involved in the dispute?
- Has the manager witnessed the conflict or only had it reported to him or her?
- Are the disputing parties peers, or does one report to the other or work in a different department?
- Is the dispute with a patient, a vendor, or another party external to the hospital?
- Does the conflict or its resolution have legal implications?

The most desired method of conflict resolution is one whereby only the parties who disagree talk with each other, accept the validity of each other's point of view, and find points of agreement that will allow them to move beyond the dispute and accomplish common goals. If the disagreement is between people who usually work well together and concerns a single issue, it can usually be settled in a calm conversation where either one convinces the other of the reasonableness of his or her position or together they find a different approach on which they agree.

In the case of Ed and Margaret, there has been too much history of their lack of cooperation to hope that a single civil conversation will resolve it. However, had each approached the other differently from the beginning, they might be working together rather than at cross-purposes.

One key to successful dispute resolution is that the parties seek understanding of each other's positions and desired outcomes. Margaret needs to appreciate Ed's history of successful financial management and learn what parts of his system are critical to maintain from his perspective. Ed needs to understand the goals of Margaret's project and be open to looking at options that would support her cost and efficiency objectives. Because they are too entrenched and angry to do this themselves at this point, the intervention of the manager or another third party will be required to resolve their differences.

Numerous third parties are available to assist with dispute resolution. However, the closer the intervener is to the warring individuals, the more likely the situation will be resolved quickly and without complications. When the disagreement is between two co-workers who report to the same person, that manager is the best individual to help them settle their differences. He or she knows both parties, has perhaps hired both of them, has helped them formulate objectives and business plans, and has an immediate vested interest in their success. Likewise, the individuals, while they may dislike each other, understand the importance of responding to a request from their manager and may be glad to have the situation contained within their department rather than having to explain themselves to others such as the legal or HR department.

Once the manager has investigated the nature and scope of the dispute by talking with the parties individually, he or she should facilitate a conversation between the two of them together. As facilitator, the manager should begin by establishing ground rules for the meeting. These rules are noted in figure 7-2.

The manager's role is to defuse the emotional aspects of the confrontation and help the individuals delineate the issues so that they can state their desired outcomes as concrete requests that can be agreed to or modified during the discussion. The manager makes it clear that he or she is neutral in this circumstance and expects the two individuals to work together toward the same objective. While the manager should not take ownership of

Figure 7-2. Ground Rules for a Conflict Resolution Meeting

As facilitator, the manager should begin a conflict resolution meeting by establishing the following ground rules:

- Each co-worker must listen to the other without interrupting.
- Each must commit to seeking a resolution to the conflict.
- Desired outcomes should start with the phrase "I wish" or "I want," not "you must" or "you should."
- All parties agree to keep the discussion confidential.

the issue, he or she should make it clear from the outset that the conflict must be satisfactorily resolved in that meeting or that several possible consequences could follow: The manager could choose and enforce a resolution that either or both might not like; he or she could "kick the issue upstairs" to the next higher level of management to settle; HR could be brought in to help facilitate a resolution; or the issue could be referred to external arbitration. While heavily entrenched individuals may welcome the escalation of the review, most prefer to see it resolved locally. All efforts should be made to resolve the problem at the lowest possible level of third-party involvement.

Having said this, at times it is valuable or even critical for the manager to solicit assistance from others. Following are some of those times:

- When the manager himself or herself is a party in the dispute
- When the involved employees are unionized or covered by a collective bargaining agreement
- When the dispute involves individuals from other departments
- When the disagreement involves a patient or patient's family
- When the dispute is with someone outside the hospital
- When the parties allege that laws or legal rights have been violated

The resources available to support the manager in these circumstances are detailed later in this chapter. But the first step in seeking additional support is to contact the HR department, where employee relations professionals can evaluate the kind of resource that would be most valuable and appropriate in each case.

Beyond local resolution, conflicts may be referred to mediation, either informal or formal, or to arbitration, where an official arbitrator makes a ruling about the dispute after hearing from both parties and reviewing submitted documentation. In most cases, the arbitrator's ruling is considered final and binding. Mediation is a process wherein a neutral third party helps those in conflict attempt to reach a resolution through facilitated dialogue, much like that described earlier in the chapter in the manager's meeting with subordinates. Mediators, however, have had specific training in conflict resolution and may be certified in the practice of mediation. Mediators and arbitrators are more likely to be seen as impartial than is the manager or another individual who works directly with the individuals involved.

Managing the Effects of Conflict on Others

Employees who work together for a significant period take on characteristics of families. Some employees nurture and protect others; some bicker; some are jealous of others' accomplishments; some become best friends both during and outside of work. Hospitals and other health care environments are typically places of teamwork and collaboration. They are also places of great intensity where all are aware of the very real life-and-death consequences of actions and decisions. When difficulty arises among co-workers, the social dynamic becomes one of tension, eroding teamwork and trust. Also, efforts to communicate and the quality of that communication drop, which can cause errors and misunderstandings. If conflict is allowed to persist, the work product and the staff are seriously affected, even if they are not immediately involved in the dispute.

Dr. Klingman reports that all the staff were watching how he would handle the conflict between Ed and Margaret. While some staff who view this dispute may be doing so out of a sense of voyeurism, most are keeping an eye on its progress because they are thinking about the impact of both the dispute and the resolution on them personally. Some may report to either Margaret or Ed and may already have sided with one or the other. Some may be offended by or disgusted with both of them. Some may be looking for radical or dramatic action by Dr. Klingman, while others will no doubt retreat to the cafeteria and hope they never have to hear anything about this issue again.

In dealing with the effects of conflict on others, the manager must take the following actions:

- Be a role model for courteous behavior, demonstrating respectful ways to discuss and resolve differences.
- Encourage employees who disagree to seek resolution, but be prepared to intervene if needed.
- Ensure confidentiality of problem-solving meetings.
- Once the conflict is resolved, assist the involved parties in communicating with other staff as necessary to restore collaborative relationships.

Above all, the manager must show that while civil disagreements are acceptable, and even encouraged when the team is working on tough problems, rude conduct and personal attacks will not be tolerated. Employees' sense of job security and dignity depend on the manager taking swift and appropriate action when conflicts arise, seeking help as necessary and assisting staff to reach a successful resolution.

Resources Available to Assist in Dispute Resolution

While some managers may more naturally fit the role of peacemaker, becoming adept at conflict management requires knowledge and skills that come with education and practice. One must be aware of the resources available to assist the manager in conflict situations and when to turn to them.

Academic institutions offer courses on conflict resolution, and the topic is usually covered in supervisory and management development programs offered in professional seminars or workshops conducted by the training and organizational development staff within the health care organization. The manager should also become familiar with relevant policies that define unacceptable conduct and its potential consequences. These policies are included in the supervisory policy manual maintained by the HR department.

Depending on the nature and severity of the conflict, the manager may contact a variety of professionals who have been specifically trained to deal with these situations. Some of these have already been mentioned: employee relations specialists in HR, certified mediators and arbitrators, and internal security staff in certain circumstances. Additionally, some organizations have internal ombudspersons who serve as neutral, confidential advisers to individuals with problems. Another confidential resource is an employee assistance program that utilizes psychologists and other skilled counselors to help troubled employees.

Figure 7-3 shows the resources available to the manager in responding to different types of conflict.

Figure 7-3. Types of Conflict and Available Resources

Types of Conflict	Available Resources
Physical altercations, threatened violence	Security, HR
Dispute involving unionized workers	HR
Manager in conflict with subordinate	Senior administrator, HR
Staff in conflict with patient or family	Senior administrator, patient advocate
Staff in conflict with external party	Legal department
Conflict involving legal claims	HR, legal department

Conclusion

Incidents involving actual or threatened violence are few, and they may not occur at all. More common is conflict in situations where co-workers do not get along or where staff poorly express disagreement with others. The manager needs to be a skilled facilitator to help resolve disputes. Just as importantly, he or she must know when to contact his or her own manager or other professional resources for assistance.

Left unchecked, conflicts intensify, and the effects can be far reaching and damaging. However difficult the situation, the manager must act swiftly and skillfully to bring about a fair and effective resolution. The productivity and morale of the staff depend on it.

8

Adapting to Being in Charge

**Help the physician manager understand
how to use authority, redefine relationships
with his or her peers, and build trust
at all levels of the organization.**

*John and I had gone to medical school together, and even though we
did our residencies at different hospitals we stayed in close touch. He
was a groomsman in my wedding, and our daughters are classmates
in middle school. When I joined City General, I introduced John
to my chief, and we were both ecstatic when he was offered and
accepted a position in the same service later that year.*

*When our chief retired and I was promoted to that position, John
and his wife, Karen, threw a celebration bash in my honor. I remember thinking how great it was to have John by my side in my new
role. But soon afterward, our relationship changed somehow, and
there was tension between us. We argued about a budget decision I
made, and I ended up telling him that since I was the one who had
to make the tough calls and live with the consequences, the least he
could do was support me. He said: "Greg, you have really changed.
I don't feel like I know you at all." Other than worrying a lot more, I
don't believe I'm any different. All I can think is that he is jealous.*

*To make matters worse, my secretary told me in confidence
that others on the staff are excluding John from some of their conversations because they think he will run right to me and report
everything they say. Now I'm really bewildered. I thought these
people liked me. What could they be saying that they wouldn't want
me to hear? And what do I do about John?*

-------------------------- Gregory Stoneman, MD, Chief, Orthopedics

Introduction

The old saying "It's lonely at the top" hits home with managers like Greg Stoneman. Newly promoted managers do not anticipate that their former peers will begin looking at them differently. They have gotten along well with their colleagues, which was likely a factor in their promotion to leadership roles. Thus, they are disappointed and somewhat shocked to discover that they are now suddenly expected to have all the answers and that staff who do not agree with a decision feel personally betrayed.

The role of manager is an occupation different from any other. It requires a special set of skills and calls for establishing relationships with subordinates where authority and decision making are clearly delineated. Inevitably, old relationships will be redefined when an individual is promoted over his or her peers or when hired from outside but perceived as a peer by those who knew him or her as a professional colleague. If handled well, this redefinition does not have to result in lost friendships or forfeited authority.

This chapter addresses four aspects of adapting to being in charge: understanding the change in roles and relationships for the new manager, becoming an inclusive manager without giving up authority, communicating in new ways, and tips for fostering positive peer relationships.

Understanding the Change in Roles and Relationships for the New Manager

A new manager is likely to experience a sense of alienation. Most people want to be liked, so the newly appointed superior may experience discomfort in making judgments about such decisions as salary or job changes that may not be well received or may negatively affect others' lives. Some new managers seek to establish their authority immediately and deliberately distance themselves from their staffs, "letting them know who is boss." They will say that they would rather be respected than popular. However, the frequent consequence is that they are feared rather than respected and that staff avoid taking problems to them or offering ideas.

Physicians appointed to management roles for the first time face even greater complexity in establishing effective working relationships with both physicians and other staff who report to them. It is not uncommon for staff to look at doctors as a kind of fraternity. Their education and training separate them from the rest of the health care community, and their strongest bonds appear to be with each other. Other clinical, administrative, and service personnel may be intimidated by them to begin with, which often comes as a surprise to physicians. In their relationships with each other, doctors are typically collegial and accustomed to conferring with each other about clinical matters. As with Dr. Stoneman, when a peer physician suddenly appears to start telling another what to do, the fraternal bond may be painfully severed.

In assuming a managerial position for the first time, one must first acknowledge that he or she is taking on a totally new job that he or she has not performed before. Just like the first time one puts a cake in the oven or drives a car, the first experience at managing other people only remotely resembles what one read in the manual or was told by teachers. The didactic educational component is critical so that one knows the expected result and what conditions are desirable to make the experience successful. But, to continue the metaphor, until one finds the cake's center gooey and the edges burned or hits the curb and flattens a tire, one will not know how to do it better the next time. Thus, the best managers are those who read and study management as a science but who understand it as an art and also analyze and learn from their experience.

Mitchell T. Rabkin, MD, president emeritus of Boston's Beth Israel Hospital, talks about management as "an intellectual enterprise." The manager, he says, must practice "metacognition"—in other words, think about what he or she is doing, reflect on what he or she has done, and consider what can be learned from that experience. When Rabkin at age thirty-five so impressed the chairman of Beth Israel's board that he was appointed president of that major Boston hospital, his only management experience had been as chief resident at Massachusetts General Hospital.

When asked how he made the leap to executive leadership with so little experience, he shakes his head at the memory of how much he had to learn. But he was a diligent student of management. Books by Wilfred Brown, Elliott Jaques, and Ralph Rowbottom were powerful in helping him understand the theoretical framework of leadership, as were the writings of management guru Peter Drucker, with whom he became personal friends. Rabkin's recommended books by these authors are listed in appendix 8-1 at the end of this chapter.

He also sought the counsel of an external consultant, Edna Homa, DBA, whom he quotes to this day. With no-nonsense wisdom, she taught him lessons that informed his leadership style. "I don't care what you do, and I don't care what you say," she told him, "but I do care that you say what you do and do what you say." Those principles of straightforward communication and integrity have been hallmarks of Rabkin's leadership for more than forty years. Another valuable mentor to Rabkin was Steve Ruma, whose PhD in clinical psychology and North End Boston street smarts helped Rabkin gain important insights into his own management thinking and actions.

In hiring his direct reports, both upon his arrival to the new role and later, he sought to bring in those who were knowledgeable and empathetic leaders from whom he could learn. Thus, all who worked directly with Rabkin followed the model he represented—the manager as constant student and teacher, roles to be exercised every day.

The steps a new manager should take to understand his or her job are summarized in figure 8-1.

Becoming an Inclusive Manager without Giving Up Authority

Inexperienced managers sometimes think they must either have all the answers to any questions that staff might raise or at least appear to have them. Perhaps overwhelmed by all the new responsibilities and not certain how staff will react to their decisions, new managers have a tendency to stay aloof and not share their own struggles to find solutions lest it look like weakness or that they were not qualified for the senior position. Quite opposite from its intended effect, this bravado is frequently interpreted by staff as arrogance or as a cover-up of bad news.

Employees look to their manager for leadership. They expect him or her to have a vision, set the direction, understand their jobs, advocate for their interests, and be available

Figure 8-1. Understanding the Management Job

The new manager adapts to being in charge by:

- Accepting that others expect him or her to have a vision and to lead them
- Preparing himself or herself and his or her staff for discussions about changed relationships
- Embracing the concept of management as an intellectual activity
- Asking mentors for recommended courses to take and books to read
- Seeking the advice of external consultants
- Having the courage to make or admit mistakes but always evaluating what he or she has learned and can teach others afterward

for support. Not only do they *not* expect the manager to have all the solutions to problems or make all the decisions but they also welcome inclusion in those processes. As Peter Drucker said, "Most discussions of decision making assume that only senior executives make decisions or that only senior executives' decisions matter. This is a dangerous mistake."[1] Drucker recognized that good decision making is important in every job because no one knows better than the individual doing the work how to improve upon it.

Not every employee should be included in every decision, of course, but the wise manager seeks input from staff who have knowledge about any component of the problem. He or she also invites questions or challenge from anyone affected by the decision. In the opening anecdote, when John disagrees with Greg Stoneman about a budget decision, Stoneman pulls rank and tells John, in effect, that his opinion does not matter because he, as manager, is the one who has to bear the consequences.

Whether or not Dr. Stoneman's budget decision was the correct one, his insistence on support for it on the basis of friendship or loyalty negates any rationality behind the decision and overlays the discussion with emotion. Rather than being a conversation about budget, it becomes a test of friendship—one that fails, from both men's point of view.

The irony is that the more the manager seeks input and debate, the more the staff respect his or her leadership. By being included in solving a problem, they recognize the importance and consequences of the ultimate decisions. They are perfectly cognizant of their manager's reasons for wanting a good outcome and become invested in the solutions.

Inclusion sounds like such a simple action, but urgency, egos, and insecurities often prevent it from happening on a day-to-day basis. The questions a manager should ask when creating plans, making decisions, and solving problems are listed in figure 8-2. The answers suggest who needs to be included in these processes.

Figure 8-2. Questions to Ask When Deciding Whom to Include in
Creating Plans, Making Decisions, and Solving Problems

1. Who has a stake in the outcome of this decision?

2. What is the best way to get information about the stakeholders' desired outcomes?

3. Which staff have expertise in this matter? Should I ask for their input on an individual or team basis?

4. What expectations should I set about including or rejecting the input I will get?

5. How should we incorporate input or advice from customers or experts outside our unit?

6. How do I acknowledge those who have helped with the resolution?

While it seems counterintuitive, the significant message here is that the more power one gives away, the more one has.

Communicating in New Ways

When Dr. Stoneman was promoted to chief of his department, he had existing relationships with the staff. He was close friends with John and felt that others liked him, too. He does not understand John's resentment of his authority and attributes it to jealousy. When he learns that other staff do not want him to know what they are talking about, he is hurt and baffled. It seems that he had been a trusted peer and friend, and now he is neither.

The importance of the new manager accepting his or her role as a unique and different job is discussed earlier. But understanding how his or her job has changed is not enough. The staff, who have been accustomed to working under someone else's direction and now sense that their world has shifted with a new leader at the helm, must also comprehend the difference. Whether this is a welcome or dreaded change, they look for clues about the manager's style and how it will affect them. Will he or she approve the flexible schedule the previous manager endorsed? Will he or she be a team player, a dictator, a prima donna, or a buddy? Is this the time to ask for that long-awaited pay raise?

If the new manager was promoted from within the staff, the staff members have preconceived notions about how he or she will interact with them. Generally they will expect the manager to relate to them as individuals much the way he or she did before the promotion. In the case of John and Greg, Greg believes that John, as a supportive friend, should simply accept his budget decision. John resents the authoritative posture assumed by Greg, clearly representing a different persona from that of his old friend. Their mutual disappointment is painful, and understandable. Such a confrontation might have been avoided had both made a more deliberate effort to understand Greg's new role and to talk candidly about how the relationship would need to be different.

How the new manager communicates with the staff early on is important in helping them make the transition to new leadership and in giving himself or herself the time to under-stand the new job and formulate plans. Figure 8-3 lists the kinds of communications that are critical in the manager's first days and weeks on the job.

Communications of the type highlighted in figure 8-3 will go a long way toward helping the manager obtain information, create trust, and establish an expectation of how interactions will occur in the future. They will not completely prevent the kind of talk that Dr. Stoneman's secretary referred to—watercooler gossip that staff would not want the manager to know. Such conversations, by the way, are typically about personal issues or bets on the Super Bowl, or someone telling a joke—topics that might embarrass the staff involved if the manager were to overhear. However, the more the manager cultivates trusting relationships, the less likely staff will worry about letting their "human side" show.

Figure 8-3. Communications for the First Weeks as a Manager

An all-hands (full staff) meeting, taking place as soon as possible:

- Allows staff to see the manager and hear about his or her background.

- Provides an opportunity for the manager to share a general vision, express confidence in the staff, and tell them what his or her broad priorities will be for the first month or so.

- If followed by a coffee hour, sets a tone of collegiality and allows the manager to greet staff in a personal and positive way.

- Invites future discussion. It may be difficult to ask for questions from your audience at this time. Most will be hesitant to speak up in front of the others. You might say something like "This is a lot to think about, but when you've done so, let me know your thoughts—either in person or by e-mail. I'll get back to you."

Individual meetings with direct reports, in their offices if possible:

- Should be a listening meeting for the manager, asking key staff members to tell him or her what they have been working on and what they see as critical issues and priorities

- Provides an opportunity for the manager to learn about staff as people—interests, hobbies, families, etc.

- Is a time to discuss when regular meetings will be held and what preparation the staff member should make for such meetings

An unscheduled walk through the departments—and that means all areas, from the operating room and intensive care unit to central supply, hospital kitchen, and laundry:

- Provides an opportunity to see all staff in their work environment and to talk with receptionists, service workers, and patients.

- Offers a chance to observe and evaluate equipment, office layout, decor, and physical comfort and convenience factors.

- Suggests that the manager will be visible and interested in the total department. Walk-throughs should be frequent so as not to be viewed as checking up or spying.

- Establishes a tone of trust and goodwill. On your way, say hello to all staff you meet, preferably by name.

Tips for Fostering Positive Peer Relationships

The physician who is newly promoted to a management position should be aware of the following dos and don'ts:

Don't become aloof or distant from your peers, but

> *Do* talk with them about how your job will require the relationship to be different.

Don't think you have to have all the answers, but

> *Do* think about whose input is necessary and valuable and how to include these individuals in decision making. Any decision of yours may favor the advice of some and not that of others. Discuss with the latter individuals why you chose not to follow their recommendations on the particular issue. Chances are they will not always be on the wrong side of your decisions, and if you follow up with them personally, they will know they have been heard and respected. Despite losing in such discussions, they will likely be winning in others and ultimately feel they are being treated fairly.

Don't assume that management is just getting along with people, but

> *Do* read widely about leadership; talk with mentors; and solicit feedback from colleagues, subordinates, and your manager about how you are doing.

The administrator who is advising the newly promoted physician manager should also be aware of certain dos and don'ts:

Don't assume that the physician's leadership and popularity in a clinical capacity will transfer with him or her into a management role, but

> *Do* plan an orientation for him or her that includes a review of job descriptions, schedules, and introductions.

Don't be intimidated by the credentials and elite status the physician has had, but

Do respect that his or her demonstrated capability to master difficult subjects is invaluable in learning how to manage. Remember that you are the teacher in this circumstance.

Don't assume that top administrators or other physicians will provide the resources and information the physician manager will need, but

Do prepare a list of courses and books that offer knowledge about leadership, as well as a list of internal resources, and *do* offer your home telephone number.

There are pitfalls that the new manager should avoid. See figure 8-4 for a brief list.

Conclusion

Becoming a manager for the first time means leaving behind the job one used to do and taking on an entirely new set of responsibilities. New physician managers in particular require a skill set that their clinical background has not given them. Making this

Figure 8-4. Pitfalls for the New Manager

The new manager can create unnecessary difficulties for himself or herself by:

- Talking negatively about the former management
- Wanting to be everyone's buddy
- Producing a five-year plan in the first week
- Hiring or firing anyone in the first month
- Thinking that a title and position give him or her respect
- Using authority in arbitrary fashion
- Staying in his or her office all the time
- Using e-mail to communicate rather than walking around and engaging staff in person
- Avoiding personal conversations about family, illness, or aspirations
- Thinking that failure is not an option

transition can be difficult and painful if neither the manager nor his or her former peers have prepared for it. Formal education in management theory is important. Critically, health care administrators and those who offer human resources services must help orient and advise the new manager. They must assist him or her realize and respect the professionalism of these and all roles in the organization so that all individuals, regardless of where they may be along the hierarchy, will feel a real part of the institution and its mission, enjoying the opportunity and the responsibility to influence to the extent their role and their capability allow.

If the manager has been promoted from within, he or she needs to talk candidly and frequently with former peers about how the changed job description will also change the relationship. It is possible to maintain friendships and still earn respect as the new boss, but only when the roles of manager and staff have been discussed and are well understood.

Reference

1. Peter Drucker, "What Makes an Effective Executive," *Harvard Business Review* (June 2004): 5.

APPENDIX 8-1

Readings Recommended by
Mitchell T. Rabkin, MD*

Wilfred Brown, *Organization*. London: Heinemann (1971). ISBN 0-435-851039.

Peter Drucker, *Management: Tasks, Responsibilities, Practices*. New York: HarperBusiness (1973). ISBN 0-7506-4389-7.

Elliott Jaques, *Requisite Organization: The CEO's Guide to Creative Structure and Leadership*. Arlington, VA: Cason Hall (1989). ISBN 0-9621070-0-X.

Elliott Jaques and Stephen D. Clement, *Executive Leadership: A Practical Guide to Managing Complexity*. Arlington, VA: Cason Hall (1991). ISBN 0-9621070-1-8.

Ralph Rowbottom et al., *Hospital Organization*. London: Heinemann (1973). ISBN 0-435-85820-3.

---

*Several of the older books have been digitized and are available on the Digital Books page of the Global Organization Design Society at http://globalro.org/index.php?option=com_content&view=category&id=10&Itemid=110&lang=en.

9

Avoiding Pitfalls and Managing Sticky Situations

Anticipate potential pitfalls, learn to
LEAP over them, and face head-on
the sticky situations that occur
in health care organizations.

This hospital drives me crazy some days. There are so many poli-cies and rules and so much paperwork. I believe I have good people instincts and make sound decisions when presented with problems. Both my intuitive sense and my ability to think quickly and analyti-cally helped me get through medical school and still contribute every day to my success as a physician and department chair. But I'm getting tripped up by the bureaucrats and the lawyers. I sometimes think they could complicate a glass of water.

For example, when my administrative assistant requested a small pay raise due to family problems, I approved it. She is a great worker and her salary is low, in my opinion. Plus, I have plenty of money in my budget to handle it. Then I hear from the HR [human resources] department: "You can't do that." I don't understand this. Isn't it my budget? Besides, I'd already promised her the raise.

I was still dealing with that situation when I heard through the grapevine that the nursing director was going to fire a longtime nurse in my department. It's true that nurses don't report to me, but this individual is a nice person. Granted, she's not the most competent nurse I've ever known, but she's been here forever. So I was glad to sign a petition along with most of the doctors in the department urging the nursing department to keep her. The next thing I know, I was summoned to the executive vice president's

*office to be told this was a bad thing to do. Since when is support-
ing a professional colleague a crime?*

*I thought I was put in this job because I'm a smart, decisive
guy. Now I'm being second-guessed all the time. They say that
doctors are arrogant, but I'm the one who is showing empathy and
compassion, and my actions are getting squelched. I guess the old
saying is right: No good deed goes unpunished.*

------------------------------ Andy Nicholas, MD, Chair, Psychiatry

Introduction

For individuals accustomed to acting independently, the com-
plexities of an organization like a hospital can frustrate them.
Physicians new to leadership roles often turn to their doctoring
knowledge rather than management skills when confronted
with problems—they see an individual who is suffering and
look for a ready cure. They do not understand why they would
need to check the policy manual or talk with someone in the
human resources or legal department before applying their rem-
edy. Indeed, health care organizations are encumbered by regu-
lations and policies, some unique to the industry and some that
apply to most employers. In addition to the plethora of relevant
federal, state, and local laws, the organizations themselves have
internal guidelines for handling employee matters. The amount
of information one needs to know to "stay out of trouble" can
be overwhelming.

Fortunately, experienced managers learn that they do not
have to know all the laws or be able to recite the policy manual. They also find that it is possible to be creative, to reward
people, and to make changes in the system by using available
sources of help and partnering with hospital colleagues with
expertise in employee matters.

This chapter addresses four aspects of avoiding pitfalls and
handling sticky situations related to managing people: recognizing an issue as a pitfall, the kinds of sticky situations that
most managers face, using available resources to avoid pitfalls

and address troublesome situations, and creating productive partnerships.

Recognizing an Issue as a Pitfall

A pitfall is a danger or difficulty that cannot be anticipated or readily recognized. Dr. Nicholas made decisions to support his administrative assistant and a nurse in his department based on a desire to help them. Both situations seemed to call for his intervention, and as department head, he felt he could offer positive solutions. Surprised and offended by the responses of others to his actions, he unintentionally stepped right into pitfalls that could have negative consequences for him and others.

The way to avoid a pitfall is to have knowledge of the probability that difficulties will occur if certain actions are taken and then choose to take another course of action. Just as a seasoned sailor learns where dangerous currents exist and avoids them, an experienced manager identifies the kinds of situations that are likely to have negative outcomes if he or she does not act with caution and knowledge.

Often one acquires this knowledge painfully. "I told Susan she could work a four-day week since she was having trouble with transportation," one manager confided. "Then three more employees wanted the same schedule and were angry when I said no. I won't make that mistake again."

This manager's pitfall is the result of failing to anticipate that her support for Susan's request has ramifications for others. She thinks that her mistake was granting the request, but the actual mistake was *how* she granted it, as will be demonstrated later in this chapter. She absolutely should help Susan in this circumstance, but she needs to do so in a way that gains others' support for an exception to general practice.

Physicians new to management are particularly prone to making promises to or deciding to hire, fire, or promote an employee without thinking about the ramifications of these actions on other people or the organization. As Dr. Nicholas states in the opening anecdote, he is sensitive to people and is confident in his ability to think quickly and analytically. However, physicians apply these skills when dealing with patients in singular situations. They would not expect to give Mrs. Miller the same diagnosis and prescription they gave Mrs. Smith; each case is viewed uniquely. But a manager's actions with an employee should not be handled in this "one-off" fashion. An experienced manager learns to think about all of his or her staff as interrelated entities and to anticipate the chain reaction created by his or her decisions.

So, other than through painful experience, how does one acquire the knowledge needed to avoid pitfalls? Some of it can be gained through formal management education and training. Educational courses or workshops in which participants review and discuss case studies that demonstrate the cause and effect of decision making are particularly helpful. Perhaps the best knowledge comes from working side by side with an experienced administrative partner. In this model of shared leadership, the physician brings his or her human sensitivities and bias for decisive action, and the nonphysician administrator contributes his or her experience with groups as well as knowledge of the policies and other available resources in the organization. Acting in tandem, they avoid pitfalls.

The Kinds of Sticky Situations Most Managers Face

No one can anticipate all the problematic situations that could arise from managing a staff, whether it consists of one person or many thousands of people. Each individual brings unique talents to the workplace. Each employee at one time or another is affected by family or financial issues, car trouble, illness, desires for vacation, promotion or retirement, and on and on. Managers often need to deal with a situation that has no direct relationship to the work of the unit but has the potential to affect it significantly. These often constitute the stickiest issues.

Earlier chapters deal with the skills needed to hire and fire appropriately and to manage both poor and good performers. Managers expect to do these tasks and can identify resources available to teach staff the needed skills and the tools to support them—it is the unexpected situations that baffle managers and leave them struggling for help. Inexperienced managers often do not recognize that they should seek help before they act, and sometimes they do not act even though they should.

Following are examples of sticky situations:

- An employee claims that a physician in your unit is making sexual advances toward her.
- You are told that an employee is putting personal mail in the stack with hospital mail to be metered.
- An employee tells you she is offended by another employee's body odor.
- An employee brings his daughter's Girl Scout cookies to the department meeting to sell to the staff.
- A nursing assistant asks you to look at some cards that he and his co-workers have signed to join a union.
- An employee's car keeps breaking down, making her late for work, and she requests a loan from the hospital to fix it.
- One of the physicians on your staff regularly goes to a neighborhood bar for lunch.
- An employee has a court-issued restraining order against her boyfriend, and she requests an escort to and from her car.
- An employee requests every Friday off to take his mother to her weekly physical therapy appointment.
- Your administrative assistant asks you to change her title to executive assistant.

These kinds of situations arise every day in organizations, yet no one manager has to deal with any one of them with enough frequency to say with certainty "I know just what to do about this." It is this uncertainty that makes the situations sticky.

What these examples have in common is that the circumstance seems unique to the individual and therefore calls for a singular response. However, experienced managers learn that, in reality, the actions they take in one situation, no matter how confidential the managers may think they are, create precedent for future actions. Another aspect of many of these situations is that the appropriate response must take into account certain laws that deal with employee rights and protections. Many managers are not aware of these laws and may inadvertently violate them even as they think they are acting in the employee's or the hospital's best interest.

Consider the implications of a manager's action in the first of the ten examples of sticky situations presented earlier: *An employee claims a physician in your unit is making sexual advances toward her.*

- Confronting the physician directly would be problematic because you do not know if the employee's claim is true or whether the physician might retaliate in some way; his reputation is at stake, as is her safety.

- Telling her to deal with it herself, saying she should "get over it," or otherwise dismissing the allegation would be wrong because employees are legally protected from harassment—sexual or otherwise—in the workplace.

- Doing nothing would also be wrong because managers are legally obligated to report claims of harassment.

The best action is to report the allegation to the HR department and assure the employee that her complaint will be investigated and that she will be protected from further harassment and/or retaliation. Human resources professionals, likely in conjunction with legal advisers, will handle the matter from this point forward in the process. The manager may need to take disciplinary action against the physician or exonerate him, depending on the findings of the investigation.

What the manager needs to know about dealing with sticky situations such as the one highlighted above is shown in figure 9-1.

The ten examples of sticky situations vary in degree of seriousness, but all require the manager to seek assistance from those professionals familiar with hospital policies on topics such as solicitation, pay and job titles, dress codes, and personal hygiene and from those familiar with laws relating to discrimination, harassment, unionization, and family and medical leaves. Sometimes handling the sticky situation is just a matter of judgment, such as dealing with the physician who goes to a bar for lunch. Even so, the wise manager seeks advice on how to handle it.

A good way to remember how to avoid trouble is found in the acronym LEAP, the process related to which is demonstrated in figure 9-2. Following this advice will help the manager leap over any pitfall.

Figure 9-1. Handling Sticky Situations

When confronted with a sticky situation:

- Do not avoid or ignore an employee complaint or request.

- Do not jump to conclusions about guilt or innocence, right or wrong.

- Treat the complaint or request respectfully and confidentially.

- Consider whether the complaint or request involves issues of fairness, discrimination, or disability, that is, those with potential legal ramifications.

- Make sure the physician manager consults with the administrative director and HR staff in a timely way.

**Figure 9-2. Avoiding Trouble in Sticky Situations:
The LEAP Mnemonic**

Listen to the request or complaint.

Expect the pitfall.

Ask for advice.

Put your trust in the experts.

Readers who want to test their knowledge of how to handle the other nine sticky situations presented earlier will find a quiz in appendix 9-1 at the end of this chapter (the answer key is provided in appendix 9-2).

Using Available Resources

This chapter's key messages to managers are to listen respectfully, avoid jumping to conclusions or taking instant action, and seek assistance from those with knowledge of the topic at hand. When it comes to sticky employee situations, the HR department contains the most knowledgeable resources. However, both physician and nonphysician managers can find numerous other sources of information and should become familiar with them. A summary of resources is noted in figure 9-3.

Figure 9-3. Available Resources in Handling Sticky Situations

1. The human resources department, for information on policies and counseling guidance

2. The legal department, for information on relevant laws and opinions on responses to potential legal hazards

3. An employee assistance program (EAP), for confidential counseling and referrals to mental health, financial, and other professional resources

4. The supervisory policy manual, for guidance on handling personnel situations in a manner consistent with hospital philosophy and practice

5. The medical staff bylaws, for understanding requirements of physician conduct

6. The hospital chaplain, for understanding religious and cultural differences and counseling support

7. The security department, for assistance in situations where conflict or violence is suspected and for recommending security measures within departments

Creating Productive Partnerships

Simply following a policy is often not a sufficient response to a situation, and complaints or requests may deserve a response not covered by policies. However, ad hoc responses need thoughtful crafting, accompanied by a clear and explicit understanding of their ramification. For instance, Dr. Nicholas's desire to give his assistant a raise deserves consideration. To be sure, the decision he made hastily to support an individual can jeopardize the fairness of pay across the organization. However, had he or his administrative manager approached HR with a request to reevaluate the job or to consider when and under what circumstances a raise might be appropriate, the physician may have been offered a workable solution, perhaps different from the one he originally sought. Human resources professionals will not reflexively squelch requests. Instead, they will collaborate to develop an action that avoids unfairness or inequity.

In the case of the manager who granted Susan a four-day workweek to help her solve a transportation problem, the decision was not wrong even though it was an exception to the policy or practice of employees working five-day weeks. It accommodated the employee in a way that helped her while also maintaining the delivery of work for the hospital. Not all requests for exceptions to policy are equally valid, and even though the manager must now consider thoughtfully each request for a four-day workweek, he or she will not have to grant them if circumstances do not present the same level of need or if the unit's ability to function is jeopardized. When one makes exceptions to policy, the rationale must be defensible and clearly communicated. Employees in general understand this. They merely want the same consideration given to others.

Susan's manager would have been wise to seek guidance from HR before granting the request. Human resources professionals have expertise in alternative work schedules and can guide the manager through the communication process. They also can help the manager think about details of the arrangement such as impact on benefits, overtime pay, and parking fees.

What seems like too much bureaucracy and paperwork to Dr. Nicholas is actually necessary process to ensure fairness and legal correctness. His sympathy with the nurse that he demonstrated by signing a petition was not necessarily misplaced, but the action both put him in a battle with administrative colleagues and potentially violated labor laws. Had he developed partnerships with those who have expertise in employee matters, his questioning of the nurse's termination would have been more thoughtful. And he might have convinced them to make a different decision or deliver it in a different way.

Conclusion

Pitfalls in managing people present themselves every day. To avoid them, managers must learn to recognize the signs of potential trouble and think about the ramifications of their decisions before taking action. While many pitfalls can be avoided through knowledge and experience, managers cannot put off responding to sticky situations. The best responses come from collaborative thinking and decision making in partnership with HR and other experts within the hospital. Remember, do not step into the pitfall, but LEAP over it.

Handling Sticky Situations Quiz

Select the best choice for the manager's response to each situation described below.

1. The manager is told that an employee is putting personal mail in the stack with hospital mail to be metered. The manager should:
   a. Contact the hospital's security department
   b. Warn the employee that she could be fired if she is doing this
   c. Attempt to catch her in the act
   d. All of the above
   e. None of the above

2. An employee tells the manager she is offended by another employee's body odor. The manager should:
   a. Ignore the complaining employee, who could be overreacting
   b. Check the policy manual to see if this topic is covered
   c. Bring in a special counselor to handle this issue
   d. All of the above
   e. None of the above

3. An employee brings his daughter's Girl Scout cookies to the department meeting to sell to the staff. The manager should:
   a. Ask him to wait to sell them until after the meeting
   b. Offer to pay for them and serve them at the meeting
   c. Allow it, knowing he or she will now need to support the Boy Scouts also
   d. All of the above
   e. None of the above

4. A nursing assistant asks the manager to look at some cards that he and his co-workers have signed to join a union. The manager should:

   a. Be polite and just look at the cards

   b. Warn him that he could be reported to the National Labor Relations Board

   c. Tell him that he or she does not believe a union is a good idea

   d. All of the above

   e. None of the above

5. An employee's car keeps breaking down, making her late for work, and she requests a loan from the hospital to fix it. The manager should:

   a. Urge her to look at other forms of transportation

   b. Look into getting her an advance on her pay

   c. Refer her to the hospital's contracted EAP

   d. All of the above

   e. None of the above

6. One of the physicians on the manager's staff regularly goes to a neighborhood bar for lunch. The manager should:

   a. Ignore the situation unless he smells of alcohol

   b. Leave literature on his desk about Alcoholics Anonymous

   c. Tell him that he or she is worried about his image in the hospital

   d. All of the above

   e. None of the above

7. An employee has a court-issued restraining order against her boyfriend, and she requests an escort to and from her car. The manager should:

   a. Tell her this is a personal matter and the hospital should not get involved

b. Offer to be her escort to and from her car

c. Arrange for the service and deduct the cost from her pay

d. All of the above

e. None of the above

8. An employee requests every Friday off to take his mother to her weekly physical therapy appointment. The manager should:

a. Suggest his mother get her treatments at the employee's hospital

b. Grant the request, but with restrictions

c. Grant the time but dock his pay

d. All of the above

e. None of the above

9. The manager's administrative assistant requests a title change to executive assistant. The manager should:

a. Make the change because it is easy to do and would make her happy

b. Refuse to make the change because she would also have to get a pay raisec. Tell her he or she suspects that she is unhappy with her job

d. All of the above

e. None of the above

Handling Sticky Situations Quiz: Answer Key

1. (a) Contact the hospital's security department

    It would be appropriate to ask security to investigate. The manager could also contact an HR professional, who would coordinate with security, the mail service, and the legal department as needed. Though the employee could be terminated for this offense, the first step is an investigation conducted by security.

2. (b) Check the policy manual to see if this topic is covered

    The employee may be overreacting, but her complaint should not be ignored. Issues such as dress, use of perfume, and personal hygiene are unpleasant to discuss, but the physical comfort of patients and co-workers must be assured. There is typically a hospital policy that establishes general standards regarding personal attire and hygiene. It is important to get advice before responding, as cultural influences, such as nationality or religion, may be a factor in these situations, but a special counselor should not be needed.

3. (e) None of the above

    Most hospitals have a no-solicitation policy that prohibits employees or outside vendors from selling products on the premises, other than those that the hospital has deemed to be in its business interest, such as the gift shop or items in the pharmacy. While selling Girl Scout cookies seems innocent, employees should be dissuaded from selling items or participating in wagering, whether in person or by way of the computer. The manager should be able to refer the employees to a handbook that covers such policies.

4. (e) None of the above

In some cases, the National Labor Relations Board has ruled that a manager's acceptance of signed union authorization cards is an acknowledgment that a union represents those employees whether or not an election has been held for employees to vote for or against unionization. While this "card check" rule is hotly debated, managers should avoid looking at cards or petitions. The employees have a right to sign cards, although the circumstances may be affected by the hospital's no-solicitation policy, and no retaliation may be taken against those who express interest in union membership. A manager can express his or her feelings about unions as long as it is not done in a threatening way; however, in this circumstance, this kind of statement is likely to invite a challenge by the union. It would be an unfair labor practice for a manager to side with a union's efforts to be recognized by the hospital.

5. (d) All of the above

The manager may indeed do all of these things. He or she should show concern for the employee's issue. Though it is improbable that the hospital would loan the employee money, it may be willing to give her a pay or vacation pay advance. The employee may also be referred to the hospital's contracted EAP, where the counselor can assist the employee in finding resources to help her with money management, though not with direct funding.

6. (c) Tell him that he or she is worried about his image in the hospital

One should not assume the doctor is drinking his lunch unless it is evident, such as by the odor of alcohol or physical or mental impairment that is related to his lunches.

There is probably no rule about where a staff person may or may not eat lunch. However, it is reasonable for the manager to be concerned about the image and reputation of his staff, so having a candid discussion with the doctor about the perception of his behavior is appropriate.

7. (e) None of the above

The employee's safety on hospital property is the organization's business. While the manager should not serve as the escort, he or she can request the assistance of the security department, which is likely to be glad to escort her. The manager should also ask security to make sure that appropriate precautions are taken within the department to shield it from any potential disturbance.

8. (b) Grant the request, but with restrictions

Under the protection of the Family and Medical Leave Act, an employee may take time from work to deal with this kind of issue. However, the amount of time an employee may take is restricted by the law, and the employer is not obligated to pay for this leave time other than through its own policies, which may allow vacation or sick time to be applied in this circumstance.

9. (e) None of the above

A manager cannot unilaterally change an employee's title. Such an action needs to be authorized by HR when it is supported by an analysis of the job compared with similar jobs elsewhere in the organization. If a title change is warranted, it may or may not be accompanied by a salary action. The employee's request does not signal unhappiness with the job, but it does suggest that he or she feels a need for recognition. The manager should explore this possibility and address the underlying causes.

10

Growing from Management to Leadership

Understand the difference between
managing and leading people,
and learn how some organizations
are educating and training physicians
to become top-flight leaders.

We all wanted to work for Dr. Charlie, but I sometimes wondered why. He was gentle and calm with his patients but a fast-paced, demanding perfectionist with the staff. He had talked the hospital into putting a clinic in the city's most dilapidated neighborhood, where drug pushers and prostitutes were both our neighbors and our patients. We worked maniacal hours, but no matter how early we arrived, Charlie was already there, and no one remembers ever leaving after he did.

I was in charge of collecting insurance co-payments when patients registered. But since almost no one had insurance, my job was largely one of filling out paperwork for the government. When I grumbled, Charlie snarled: "You want to do something meaningful? Come up with some ways to help these folks." Taking him at his word, I planned a health fair to be held on the street with free screenings for various diseases, nutrition counseling, and health education for teens. The staff loved the idea, but we had no way to pay for it.

Charlie groused: "I have to do everything around here." But he went to his wealthy patients whom he saw at the hospital, and within a week, we had more than enough funds for the fair. In fact, he talked the hospital into donating everything we needed, and he used the philanthropic dollars to seed his next idea—another clinic in another bad neighborhood.

When Charlie died, elaborate memorials were held at the hospital and at his medical school. We read a long obituary in the local press. It said he held a patent for a medical device he invented, he was on a school board, and he had received a Purple Heart for his service in the army. We never knew any of those things. But we think he would have been proudest of the tribute scrawled on cardboard and left by the heap of flowers at our clinic's door. It read: "Doc C—you saved our life."

-------------- Amanda Chen, Business Manager, Jones Corner Clinic

Introduction

Are all good managers leaders? Is there a difference between managing and leading? The previous chapters present responsibilities of managers in directing and supporting the work of other people. They put forth the notion that effective managers gain the trust of their subordinates through hiring the right people, planning and delegating well, evaluating and rewarding appropriately, firing when necessary, avoiding pitfalls, and developing their staff while supporting the health care organization's mission. Is there something that leaders do that good managers may not?

This chapter explores several aspects of leadership in health care: the differences, if any, between managers and leaders; the leader's role in driving change; resources for leadership development; how health care systems and hospitals are thinking about leadership; the story of a hospital committed to developing leaders; and tips for helping physicians become great managers and leaders.

The Differences, if Any, between Managers and Leaders

Many management and leadership gurus have commented on the distinction between these roles:

Management is doing things right; leadership is doing the right things.
> —*Peter Drucker, author*

Management is about arranging and telling. Leadership is about nurturing and enhancing.
> —*Thomas J. Peters, author*

Managers are oriented to process, while leaders are attuned to substance. . . . Managers tend instinctively to delegate; leaders like to get involved in working toward solutions to substantive problems.
> —*Abraham Zaleznik, Professor of Leadership Emeritus,*
> *Harvard Business School*

Management is a position that is granted; leadership is a status that is earned.
> —*K. Scott Derrick, Director of Professional Development,*
> *Senior Executives Association*

Management works in the system; leadership works on the system.
> —*Stephen Covey, author*

The point here is not to quibble over definitions but to recognize that some aspects of leadership do not fit tidily into the day-to-day functions of management covered in earlier chapters. These aspects have to do with having a vision, articulating an aspirational goal, and inspiring others to take actions they would otherwise not take. Because that vision is of an ideal or a place where the organization has not been before, the leader must demonstrate the positive possibilities of change. Leaders are often able to motivate others to try new approaches or take risks by infecting them with their passion for a cause.

Harvard Business School Professor John Kotter said: "I have found that people who provide great leadership are also deeply interested in a cause or discipline related to their professional arena. . . . Such leaders also tap deep convictions of others and connect those feelings to the purpose of the organization; they show the meaning of people's everyday work to that larger purpose."[1]

Physicians appointed to management jobs have a ready platform from which to become great leaders. While any person in any role can exercise leadership, physicians inspire awe in those around them because they know so much science yet are artists in their craft and are healers and savers of lives. Whether the physicians are cantankerous and curmudgeonly or soft-spoken and gentle, their staff and patients look to them for wisdom, expecting them to have answers and to offer a sense of direction.

Yet it would be a mistake for physicians to assume that their training and knowledge are sufficient to make them effective leaders or for staff to confuse a physician's aura with the ability to make him or her—or the organization—successful. As Drucker says, "Leadership is not about a list of attributes as no two leaders will exhibit the same list, nor is it about charisma or some king-like quality. It is all about delivery of performance. Just like management."[2]

Thus, while physicians may be in a position to lead others to a course of action, they need to be able to translate their vision and passion for a cause into a plan that people can follow. And they, or others at their direction, must use finely honed management skills to ensure that the plan is executed effectively. In other words, they need to hire people with the right skills, delegate the necessary tasks, and evaluate both the work of the staff and the effectiveness of the plan, taking corrective actions along the way.

The most successful organizations are those in which leadership attributes and management skills combine to achieve results. These organizations are also characterized by continuously raising the bar on performance, where leaders challenge themselves and others to take risks and make changes to improve the quality and efficiency of their services.

The Leader's Role in Driving Change

Despite people's desire to see improvements in their organizations, they seldom like the process of getting there. Change is difficult because it makes us uncomfortable and requires us to accept the notion that some future possibility is worth risking our present sense of security. Though a leader's vision may be appealing, staff may well ask: "If that vision is realized, how will it affect my job, my relationship with my peers, my career goals?"

Sarah O'Neill reflected on the vision of Tom Delbanco, MD, who headed Beth Israel Hospital's primary care department, where she served as administrative director. "He was always thinking about what patient care would look like in the future. When he recruited new doctors, he was not looking just at the strengths we needed then, but at what kind of research and talent we would need in the years ahead." Sometimes the vision frightened staff, particularly those who were averse to change. And sometimes, she said: "We had to bring him down to earth and think about how to do things practically." But over the years she worked with Delbanco, O'Neill increasingly appreciated the importance of his vision and plans for the future. "He helped us stick with the goal and remember what we were trying to achieve. We always knew what we wanted to accomplish. It was exciting. It motivated us. 'We can be ahead of everyone else,' we said and believed."

In addition to articulating a vision, the most notable trait of great leaders, according to John Kotter, is "their quest for learning. They show an exceptional willingness to push themselves out of their own comfort zones, even after they have achieved a great deal. They continue to take risks, even when there is no obvious reason for them to do so. . . . Often they are driven by goals or ideals that are bigger than what any individual can accomplish, and that gap is an engine pushing them toward continuous learning."[3]

Physicians typically demonstrate another set of characteristics that can reduce their management effectiveness but make them successful leaders: autonomy and independence. Harvard Business School Professor Emeritus Abraham Zaleznik said: "Leaders have to achieve psychological independence to enable them to apply their talents to the work at hand."[4] And another Harvard Business School professor, Bill George, said: "[Leaders] who are too responsive to the desires of others are likely to be whipsawed by competing interests, too quick to deviate from their course or unwilling to make difficult decisions for fear of offending."[5]

Michael Rosenblatt, MD, former dean of Tufts University School of Medicine, said that he, like most physicians, emerged from medical school believing he could do anything, including running a large organization. "Some experience as a manager quickly demonstrated that I didn't know as much as I thought," he said. "I believed you were either born a people person or you weren't. I was surprised to learn that there are principles and science underlying management." However, though physicians are often labeled as arrogant, it is that self-confidence and willingness to step into unknown territory that are hallmarks of leaders.

Figure 10-1 lists the traits of leaders that are different from those of managers.

Figure 10-1. Traits of Leaders That Are Different from Those of Managers

Great leaders are known for:

- Focusing on the future
- Exhibiting passion for a cause
- Articulating a vision
- Driving change to achieve the vision
- Seeking continuous learning
- Acting with autonomy and independence

Effective managers are often superb leaders as well, which means they exhibit the leadership traits cited in figure 10-1 but also perform the functions of good management. These talented individuals often become hospital presidents, chief operating officers, or heads of major services, taking their organization to new heights and ensuring the delivery of exceptional patient care. Frequently, these leaders partner with capable administrators who share the vision and translate it into action.

Resources for Leadership Development

A quick Internet search for the term *leadership institutes* yields 10,300,000 entries. An institute to develop leadership capabilities exists for women in the media, another for under-represented minority scientists, yet another to train and place conservatives within the public policy process, and many thousands more.

An advanced search for the term *leadership institutes for physicians* reduces the number of entries to 470,000. One can enroll in degree or certification programs, attend executive training classes, take online leadership courses, or attend any one of thousands of seminars devoted to the topic of leadership. Clearly there is no dearth of educational resources for physicians seeking to become leaders or to improve their skills.

Many of these programs are designed for physicians interested in leadership in a particular role or setting. The Institute for Medical Leadership, for example, tailors workshops to the unique interests and needs of an individual health care organization. It offers chief of staff boot camps as well as board retreats and physician and executive coaching. Another example is the Biomedical Enterprise Program, which is jointly administered by the Harvard University–Massachusetts Institute of Technology (MIT) Division of Health Science and Technology and the MIT Sloan School of Management. This program's Web site, http://bep.mit.edu, states that it "prepares tomorrow's entrepreneurs and managers to transform scientific discovery into patient-oriented, commercially successful products and services."

Similarly, a search for books on leadership for physicians brings forth just fewer than 2 million entries. On the Web site of Pam Pohly Associates (www.pohly.com), a health care consulting and executive search firm, one can find a list of 179 books that are recommended on the topic of leadership development for physicians. Following are examples of these offerings:

Physicians as Leaders: Who, How, and Why Now? by Mindi K. McKenna and Perry Pugno (Radcliffe-Oxford, 2005)

Leading Transformational Change: The Physician-Executive Partnership by Thomas A. Atchison and Joseph S. Bujak (Health Administration Press, 2001)

The Physician Manager's Handbook: Essential Business Skills for Succeeding in Health Care, 2nd ed., by Robert Solomon (Jones & Bartlett, 2007)

In a December 2009 *Wall Street Journal* article, Jane Porter cites a growing trend in business schools offering programs targeted at physicians. For example, Harvard Business School began a nondegree program in October 2009 that consists of three, one-week courses spread over nine months. The University of Pennsylvania's Wharton School of Business conducts the Penn Medicine Leadership Forum and has expanded its curriculum to include projects across the health system's three hospitals. Porter also notes that Duke University's Fuqua School of Business planned to launch a master's degree program in 2010 focusing on how new technology can be used to improve patient care. Vanderbilt University began a year-long master's program in health care management, and Dartmouth College's Tuck School of Business is exploring joint degree and nondegree programs with the Dartmouth Institute for Health Policy and Clinical Practice.[6]

These programs and the earlier-mentioned books may or may not be better than others available, but they are examples of the breadth and depth of resources physicians and health care organizations may tap. They also reflect the growing awareness that physicians and hospitals can be more effective when they apply some principles of successful businesses.

Additionally, many hospitals and health systems offer internal workshops and seminars on leadership for physicians and staff. They also design on-boarding processes that help new physician leaders launch their tenure in a successful environment, and many assign mentors or other colleagues to support physician managers as they start their new roles.

Figure 10-2 summarizes the types of resources available to physicians for leadership development.

How Health Care Systems and Hospitals Are Thinking about Leadership

As hospitals employ more physicians, they recognize that these doctors need to embrace the mission and culture of the organization, collaborate with providers and staff across multiple disciplines and departments, and be responsive to the challenges and priorities established by the hospital's leadership.

Figure 10-2. Resources for Leadership Development

1. Academic business schools offering both degree and certification programs in leadership
2. Professional seminars and workshops offered by leadership institutes
3. Online leadership courses
4. Executive coaches
5. Books and professional periodicals
6. Internal training and development programs
7. On-boarding and orientation processes
8. Mentors

"We hire for fit," says Judy Hodgson, senior vice president for culture and people at PeaceHealth, a health care system with hospitals and medical groups in Oregon, Washington, and Alaska. The organization's culture is so strong and well defined that not everyone can be successful there. Employees, and especially those hired as managers, must possess certain core values and demonstrate key attributes, including being a team player and collaborator. Hodgson says the corollary to the organization's hiring policy is that it also "fires for fit." Physicians who are arrogant or treat people disrespectfully are not considered a fit at PeaceHealth if they are unable to change their behaviors. Hodgson says that she has been extremely lucky to have chiefs of staff who have been willing to stand side by side with her in working with physicians and staff to ensure that negative behaviors are proactively and thoughtfully addressed.

The same theme is echoed by Brandon Melton, senior vice president of human resources for the Lifespan health system in Rhode Island. "Physicians who are successful leaders here," says Melton, "are not driven by ego or a need to take credit. They have a high degree of emotional intelligence and act in the interest of the patients and the organization." Melton describes a physician leader with excellent credentials whom Lifespan recruited from outside the organization. "He was disruptive and disrespectful of his peers and subordinates." Apparently, his previous employer had tolerated his attitude. "This physician's behavior was inconsistent with our organization's values for respect and fairness, and he was not used to being confronted," says Melton. "After a period of time he left for another opportunity."

The Story of a Hospital Committed to Developing Leaders

Hospitals are increasingly conscious that achieving the highest level of quality in the delivery of patient care—and ensuring their competitive success—depends on empowering employees to identify and correct errors, to create efficiencies in systems and processes, and to ensure that improvements are sustainable. These activities in turn rely on leaders at all levels of the organization understanding these objectives, knowing the techniques for implementing them, and engaging their employees in carrying them out.

As indicated earlier, multiple resources exist to help individuals develop leadership skills. However, few health care organizations exhibit the kind of "full-court press" in developing leaders that is applied at the Beth Israel Deaconess Medical Center (BIDMC) in Boston.

In a city that is often referred to as "the Mecca of medical care," BIDMC seeks to differentiate itself from the myriad teaching and community hospitals in Boston on the basis of quality and service to patients. These ideals are common to the mission statements of hospitals everywhere, but BIDMC has worked to fulfill them by establishing a highly intensive, multi-pronged approach to developing its present and future leaders.

Jo Ayoub, director of organizational development at the medical center, talks about the Sloane Fellows Program as one of the significant initiatives to develop its leaders. Named after Carl Sloane, a former chairman of the board of trustees, and led by Amy Wasserman, program manager for leadership development, it is an intense eighteen-month program designed to identify and develop the next generation of leaders. Approximately twenty "emerging leaders" are nominated by physician chiefs and administrators to participate in a program that incorporates didactic and experiential learning. A recent graduating class included three physicians along with high-potential directors and middle managers.

Each participant completes a 360-degree evaluation at the onset of the course. This tool requires the individual to rate himself or herself relative to competencies the hospital has identified as critical to its leaders. The fellow also asks several others to rate him or her on these competencies. Typically, the raters include one's immediate manager, several subordinates, and some peers. Working individually with a coach and his or her immediate manager, the participant develops an action plan to improve in the areas indicated by the evaluation.

Ayoub says the 360-degree feedback process for physicians has been vital in helping them understand the competency of "influence in leading change." "It's about putting themselves out there to ask for feedback. These leaders says things like 'This is the first time I've been validated; I never knew I made my staff feel appreciated.'"

The fellows also gain understanding of themselves through use of the Myers-Briggs Type Indicator® (MBTI) assessment. Based on the psychological types described by C.G. Jung, the MBTI is a personality inventory that reveals individual preferences in one's perceptions and judgments. Additionally, the program includes readings on leadership and discussions led by Harvard Business School faculty.

The fellows work on two big projects during the course of the program. At the conclusion, participants undergo a post-program 360-degree evaluation to gauge any changes in perceptions of their competencies. As her project, one of the Sloane fellows developed a 360-degree feedback instrument just for physicians that will be piloted within a specific clinical department.

The program is so popular that Ayoub says she gets many calls from physicians and others who want to become Sloane fellows.

Beth Israel Deaconess Medical Center, as one of many hospitals committed to developing leaders, is an excellent model for identifying physicians who can become effective administrators. As Ayoub says, "When we give these docs the opportunity to teach us and engage in conversation, they become colleagues. When we treat them as separate, that's how they behave. Physicians want to be involved, want to help."

Tips for Helping Physicians Become
Great Managers and Leaders

Much of this book is devoted to providing advice to help physicians become effective managers and the resources available to them and their organizations toward that end. However, there is widespread belief that the best leaders have some innate qualities that are fundamental to their success.

Judy Hodgson says that PeaceHealth's best physician leaders come to their jobs with "a servant's heart." The patient is central to every act and decision. "There is something in their DNA," she says, "that gives them this bias." Brandon Melton describes two effective physicians leaders, coincidentally both women raised in rural areas, who bring their values to the job: "They are both generous, cooperative, and respectful to everyone. I'm sure they've been this way since they were young children. Our employees so admire them, they would follow them into the Narragansett Bay."

Both Hodgson and Melton talk about other traits, such as a willingness to take risks, to admit mistakes, to never blame others, and to do what is best for their patients and the organization even if it means sacrificing personal interests. Yet these health systems, like hospitals across the country, are supporting massive numbers of workshops, training programs, and seminars on leadership. They send their managers to the degree and nondegree programs mentioned earlier. They believe fervently that the best can be made better.

What is clear is that no silver bullet exists to create and sustain strong leadership. Rather, a health care organization must employ a multiplicity of initiatives that stem from an understanding of the culture one has or wants to create and a willingness to support an individualized approach to the education and development of its managers and leaders.

Figure 10-3 presents tips for helping physicians be great managers and great leaders.

Figure 10-3. Tips for Helping Physicians Be Great Managers and Great Leaders

Organizations can help physicians grow their management and leadership capacities by:

- Identifying the skills and knowledge gaps that exist when physicians are hired or promoted into management jobs
- Identifying and hiring for the values and personal characteristics that are consistent with the organization's culture
- Preparing a personal development plan for each physician manager
- Committing resources to educational support
- Offering reward and recognition programs to honor achievement in personal development
- Conducting succession planning to keep good managers engaged and prepared for future opportunities

Conclusion

Health care organizations are complicated and labor-intensive institutions. They are also in fierce competition for patients and for reimbursement from payers. Each seeks to operate in ways that are efficient, are financially viable, and produce high-quality service to patients. Effective management is required at every level; even more important are first-rate leaders—individuals who envision a constantly improving medical facility and who use their own talents and passions to engage staff in achieving that vision.

By the time physicians step into executive positions in health care or other industries, they have traveled a long distance. They have succeeded as scholars, researchers, authors, and caregivers—all before becoming responsible for organizational results. So why do they take on the challenges and inevitable headaches of managing finances, facilities, and people? With their passion for constantly improving the patient experience, they willingly dive into the world of education again—this time to learn the skills of management and to emerge as leaders of the most vital services to humanity.

References

1. John Kotter, "Winning at Change," *Leader to Leader* 10 (fall 1998): 27–33.

2. Peter Drucker, *Management: Tasks, Responsibilities, Practices* (New York: Harper Collins, 1999).

3. Kotter, "Winning at Change."

4. Martha Lagace, "The Inner Life of Leaders: Q&A with Abraham Zaleznik," *HBS Working Knowledge* (August 13, 2008) [http://hbswk .hbs.edu/item/5970.html]. Accessed June 7, 2010.

5. Bill George, "The Journey to Authenticity," *Leader to Leader* 31 (winter 2004): 29–35.

6. Jane Porter, "Doctors Seek Aid from Business Schools," *Wall Street Journal* (December 22, 2009): A31.

Index